To

From

Richard Boston

**Starkness
At Noon**

Starkness At Noon

Richard Boston

Five Leaves Publications

Starkness At Noon

*Published in 1997 by Five Leaves Publications,
PO Box 81, Nottingham NG5 4ER*

*Five Leaves Publications
receives financial assistance from*

EAST
MIDLANDS
ARTS

*Copyright: Richard Boston
Cover photograph: Nobby Clarke
Design by 4 Sheets Design & Print
Printed in Great Britain by Anthony Rowe*

ISBN 0 907123 32 5

Contents

Foreword   1

People
  The Postman Horse   3
  Out In The Mid-day Sun   13
  Jobs for the Boys   16
  Paul, Emile and Aix   25
  Buckminster Abbey   37
  The Game of the Name   42

Books
  The Young Aviator   46
  William the Conqueror   63
  In the Garden of Giorgio Bassani   75

Against The Stream
  The Best Air in the World   84
  Mere Anarchy   91
  The Candidate   118
  Land of Lost Horizons   157

Good Grief
  Knees up Charlie Brown   160
  Baxter Basics   168

Home and Abroad
  Bologna   173
  A Very Still Life   193
  Change in the Village   201
  Starkness at Noon   209

FOREWORD

The pieces of writing assembled here are on a variety of subjects and were written over a long period of time. In one of them the late Buckminster Fuller discusses synergy. This is when two or more items together produce an effect that is greater than the sum of their individual effects. The first task of a Foreword such as this is to help the reader (or reviewer) by identifying this synergy in what would otherwise merely be (in the words of Juvenal) *nostri farrago libelli,* our little hotchpotch of a book. (A spot of Latin is OK in a Foreword, if not *de rigeur:* if nothing else it shows you own a copy of the *Oxford Dictionary of Quotations*).

So what I must now do is show how these bits and pieces, when taken together, in some complex and subtle way constitute a unified and coherent whole.

Consider it done.

The second job is to say something about the text. The earliest of the pieces collected here are nearly 30 years old and were written for a periodical, *New Society,* which sadly no longer exists, its marsupial survival in *New Statesman and Society* now being purely nominal. The rest first appeared in the *Guardian* over the past dozen years or so. Writing from the period in between has already found its way into book form in *Beer and Skittles* and *Baldness Be My Friend* (both out of print) or still lies undisturbed in such copies as survive of my own short-lived magazines, the *Vole* and *Quarto.* For the purposes of this book, I have made a number of corrections and additions, restored some cuts and made others, but for the most part I have left them as they first appeared. This has inevitably led to occasional minor repetitions from one piece to another. Readers who find them obtrusive are to be congratulated on the closeness of their attention

My final task is the pleasant one of expressing heartfelt thanks to all and sundry, which I hereby do — especially to Nobby Clarke for the photograph on the front cover and to George Melly for the puff on the back; to Ian Mayes, Jeanette Page, Deborah Orr, Helen Oldfield and Alan Rusbridger at the *Guardian;* to Ross Bradshaw of Five Leaves, who suggested the book and can therefore take the blame; to my father for his recollections about his flying days, and for much else; to Marie Claude; to many friends; and to Frédéric Chopin, Eric Satie, Dolly Parton, Bela Bartok, Fats Waller, Pinetop Smith, Georges Brassens, Jo Stafford, Frankie Laine, Roy Orbison, Duke Ellington, Cow Cow Davenport, Sonny Rollins and Josephine Baker for the sound-track.

THE POSTMAN HORSE

Le Facteur Cheval is not well known even in France, and when you mention his name people find it funny. The Postman Horse sounds a bit like Jacques Tati's bicycling postman in *Jour de Fête,* but he was a real man and the reason why he was called by this name is simple. Just as the Douanier Rousseau had worked as a Customs officer, so Joseph Ferdinand Cheval (as unusual a surname in French as Horse is in English) was *un facteur*, a postman.

Certainly he worked like a horse. "If anyone wants to show more determination than me, they'd better get on with it," he said. He was born in 1836 in Charnes-sur-Herbasson, in the Drôme, east of the Rhône, north of Romans-sur-Isère, which is on the way from Valence to Grenoble. After a childhood in the extreme poverty prevalent in agricultural France of the time, he worked for a baker, knocked about a bit, for a while was virtually a tramp, and there are some years unaccounted for. He seems to have spent most of his time day-dreaming.

In 1869 he became postman of the village of Hauterives about five miles from where he was born. His mail delivery every day was a 20-mile round trip on foot over rough country. While it was physically hard going it gave plenty of time for day-dreaming.

When he was 40, and like Dante in the middle of the road of life *(Nel mezzo del cammin di nostra vita)*, he tripped over a stone. What the apple was to Newton, or the kettle to James Watt, or the bath to Archimedes, this stone was to the postman. Cheval looked at it and was intrigued by the shape. He thought about the stone, and returned to the spot and found other stones with even more curious shapes, eroded by the elements over centuries. He found more and more stones in river-beds and on the hillsides, fossils and shells from the sea-beds of millennia ago. He put them in his pockets, then he carried them in bags, and when there were too many for the bags he left them in heaps and collected them later with his wheelbarrow. That wheelbarrow was the only help he ever had.

His thoughts seem to have run along lines something like this. These stones have curious shapes. They were made by nature. If nature can make curious shapes, then so can Ferdinand Cheval. And after all those years of dreaming, the time had come to turn dreams into reality.

Events were given a further shove by the death of his first wife and his second marriage in 1878. The second Madame Cheval was illiterate (the illiteracy rate in the region was so high that one wonders who read or wrote the letters the Facteur walked so far to deliver). Be that as it may, she had a small dowry which Cheval spent on buying a plot of land. On this, in the same year that his daughter was born, he began to build in 1879.

He was a small man, with a rather distrustful expression, very tough and (as he said) very, very determined. "I was the first to agree with those who called me insane," he said. "I was not a builder, I had never even handled a bricklayer's trowel. I wasn't a sculptor, I'd never even used a chisel. I knew nothing about architecture and it is a subject on which I am still ignorant."

Every day started with the 20-mile postal round. When the day-job was done, he got down to work on the Palace, the Palais Idéal, for eight or more hours, sometimes with another few hours' walk to collect stones from his heaps. He worked by candlelight way into the night, and often got up at two or three in the morning.

In 1896 he retired as postman at the age of 60. From then on it was building full-time. In 1905 an article in *Le Matin* for the first time brought his work to the attention of anyone outside the village, but the final stones were not laid until 1912. Single-handedly he had created an edifice 26 metres by 14, and nearly 11 metres (34 foot) high. He had used 3,500 bags of lime and cement, and it had taken him (as he recorded on a wall of the building) 10,000 days, 93,000 hours, 33 years work. Clearly his challenge to anyone to show comparable determination was in no sense an idle one.

By now he had surely more than earned himself a rest — after all he was born three years before Cézanne — but at the age of 74 he started work on an enormous family vault in the village cemetery. He managed to complete this before he was finally put to rest in it when he died in 1924 at the age of 88.

Rather late in the day he was discovered by André Breton and became greatly admired by the surrealists. In 1969 André Malraux as Minister of Arts called the Palais Idéal a unique example of Art Naif and had it listed as a historic monument. And what greater honour to the memory of the old postman than for his work to be on a postage stamp? One honour only, perhaps. In the same year, 1984, a statue to the Facteur Cheval was put up outside the village post office of Hauterives, where in his lifetime he had been treated with little short of derision. The Palace had begun to delapidate but after ten years of repairs and restoration it was opened to the public in 1995.

To say that the place is extraordinary is a feeble understatement, but no word or words can be adequate for a place which is to be experienced rather than described. Perhaps Coleridge in laudanum-fuelled Khubla Khan-mode could have done justice to this — well, this stately pleasure-dome. It's a bit Arab mosque, a bit Hindu temple, and Cambodian, and Egyptian; there's a castle here, a chalet there, there are bits of all sorts and they somehow add up. There are sculpted deer, dogs, crocodiles, elephants, camels and angels. And presiding over all, and protecting the entrance, are three huge figures of (in Cheval's words) Julius Caesar the Roman conqueror, Vercingetorix the defender of Gaul, and Archimedes the great Greek man of science.

These figures are as elongated as any by Giacometti, but not gaunt or angular. If anything their contours are rounded, and their pebble-dash texture gives them a knitted appearance. They wear funny hats, and on their spindly legs there are something like plus-fours. By any standards they ought to be ridiculous, but instead they contrive to be impressive, dignified and friendly. Between them stand the Druid Goddess Veleda, and the Egyptian Goddess Isis. And all around there are towers and pinnacles, tunnels and caves and grottoes, vaults, stairs, crenellations and aloes and semi-tropical trees made of cement.

The images are assembled with the all-embracing (though not indiscriminate) hospitality of an autodidact. Images and references are taken from all nations, all religions, all cultures. Here the lamb may lie down with the lion and sleep safe and sound. Scattered over the walls are words of wisdom as homespun as poker-work:

> The weak and the strong are equal in the face of death.
>
> The dying man is a setting star that rises more brightly elsewhere.
>
> The dead are not absent but invisible.
>
> To the brave, nothing is impossible.
>
> In the minutes of leisure my work has allowed me I have built this palace of One Thousand and One Nights and carved out my memory.
>
> Winter and summer, night and day, I have walked, I have roamed the plains, the hillsides and the rivers, to bring back hard stones chiselled by nature. My back has paid for it. I have risked everything, even death.
>
> This monument is the work of a country person.

> Remember that to want something is to be able to do it.

> Help yourself and heaven will help you.

There is a constant emphasis on equality. The high and mighty are equal with the humble and meek, all the beasts of the field and the fowls of the air, all religions, all beliefs are equal. And so is the partnership in endurance shared by Cheval and his wheelbarrow. Most touchingly he has built a grotto to enshrine the wheelbarrow, his saw and trowels. The wheelbarrow speaks on behalf of the other tools:

> 1906. I am the faithful companion of the intelligent worker who every day fetched from the countryside what he needed. Now his work is finished, he is at rest from his labour and I, his humble friend, have the place of honour.

Then, it seems, all the tools speak together in honour of Monsieur Cheval:

> We say to future generations that you alone built this temple of marvels. The purpose was to show what could be done by sheer willpower, the possibility of overcoming mental and material obstacles. All civilisations and religions express the same great sentiments, the unity of the works of man and nature.

Cheval was not only a great sculptor-architect. He was also quite an engineer. Since the surfaces of the building are all covered with decoration it is hard to see quite how the structure works but as you walk about it, under it and over it, the whole thing feels absolutely sound, and it is a very big building. I would welcome expert opinion on this but it seems to me that Cheval was using reinforced concrete some time before it is supposed to have been invented. There's no doubt that a lot of cement has gone into it. The prevailing greyness that is the result looks just right, but the general lack of colour may also be explained by the fact that he worked so much by candle-light at night.

Near the Palace, Cheval built a garden house where he could sit at sunset and look at his great work, and doubtless think up more adages to write on its walls.

> Remember that you are dust and that only your soul is immortal.
>
> God protects genius.
>
> This marvel, of which the maker can be proud, is unique in the universe.
>
> The child arrives in life with hands full of future. If he knows what to do he leaves with them full of memories.
>
> My will-power has been as strong as this rock.
>
> To get where you want you have to be pig-headed.
>
> Time doesn't pass; we do.

It could all so easily be absurd, but it is magnificent. The atmosphere is mysterious but in spite of all the dark grottoes and caves it is never threatening. There are no horrors. It is certainly the stuff that dreams are made on, but not nightmares.

I have the feeling that unlike almost any other great artist, Cheval was a good man. If Cheval wasn't a great artist then words have no meaning. If he wasn't a good man, then nothing has any meaning.

Cheval anticipated Dali and Gaudi and much else in 20th century art. If by conventional standards he was a bit cracked, then it is too bad for conventional standards. He was cracked like the Douanier Rousseau, and William Blake and Christopher Smart, and in a mad world it is people such as them who are sane. Those of us who think we are not cracked have much to learn from them, and from children and animals.

Another who belongs in that company is Raymond Isidore.

As with Cheval, the main events of his life can be summarised with a few dates. He was born in Chartres in 1900, spent his whole life in Chartres and died there in 1964. He served an apprenticeship in a foundry, but for most of his life worked as a sweeper in the town cemetery. In 1924 he married a widow who was eleven years older than himself and had three children.

In 1928 Isidore bought a scrap of land on the outskirts of the town and started building his house. He had hardly any money and (like Cheval) no help other than that of his wheelbarrow and his own two hands (we have Madame Isidore's word for it that her two sons never did a stroke). He found his building materials where he could, scavenging even the pieces of marble that make the foundations.

After four years he had built three small rooms. This was enough for preparing and eating meals, and for a bed to sleep in: Isidore reckoned that these were the basic requirements for happiness. He thought a lot about happiness. As he said, "I think too much. At night I think about people who are wretched. I would like to tell them about the spirit which told me how to embellish life. Many people could do as much but they haven't the wish to. I have used my hands and they have made me happy. We're not living in a very good century. I would like to live among flowers and in beauty. I'm looking for a way to get people out of misery."

He bought an adjacent parcel of land, making a long narrow site twelve yards wide and a full 50 yards long.

There were gardens for flowers and vegetables, and the rabbits and hens. And the building went on — a chapel, a workshop, a privy, and walls and walkways and arches.

Throughout this time he was collecting like a jackdaw — broken bottles, pieces of flint, old clocks, porcelain, broken plates and cups and saucers, anything durable, and preferably brightly coloured or patterned. He did this without any apparent end in view, just piling the fragments in heaps. Then in 1938 (nearly the same age as when Cheval had his toe-stubbing enlightment) he had an idea. In his own account, "I built my house first of all to put a roof over our heads. I had gone for a walk in the fields when by chance I saw little bits of broken glass, fragments of china, broken crockery. I gathered them together, without any precise intention, for their colours and their sparkle. I picked out the good stuff and threw away the bad. I piled them up in a corner of my garden, and then the idea came to me to make a mosaic of them to decorate my house. To start with I thought I would just decorate part of the walls. I often walked miles to find my material; the broken plates, bottoms of perfume bottles, medicine bottles, things that people don't want and throw away in quarries and rubbish dumps but that are still useful. I took the things that other people throw away. So many things are thrown away that could be used to give life and happiness."

From his heaps of unconsidered trifles he made art. He was an avid Bible-reader and must surely have remembered the verse in Psalm 118: "The stone which the builder refused is become the head-stone of the corner." It was true not only of his pioneering recycling but of his attitude to human life. He said of his employment as a cemetery sweeper that it was as though he'd been "thrown on the rubbish-dump of the dead, when I was capable of doing other things, as I have proved." For Isidore there was no such thing as rubbish, material or human: rejects can be made into things of beauty.

His single-minded collecting is what led to his being called Picassiette. This is quite a clever name. The Picasso of plates, but in the dictionary *picassiette* means a scrounger — not a pickpocket but a pickplate. But Isidore didn't pick from plates, he picked the plates themselves.

When he had done the walls of the house, inside and out, he just kept going, covering everything with mosaics, the walls, the floors, the paths, the ceilings, the courtyards, the chapel, the summerhouse and finally the furniture itself, the wheelbarrow, the flowerpots, the stove, the bed and even the radio.

The buildings, rooms, walls and garden that Picassiette created are in their way as encyclopedically rich as Chartres cathedral itself. All creation is here, in gorgeous colour, with the blue of the cathedral glass predominant. What Chartres cathedral does in glass and sculpture, Isidore did after his fashion in mosaic. There's fish, flesh and fowl, butterflies, dogs, cats, giraffes, camels and every manner of living thing. There are monuments, castles, cathedrals and thrones. There are the rose windows of Chartres, all the houses and streets of Chartres and on the sky-line of the wall the very cathedral itself.

The richest man in the world couldn't possibly afford what Isidore owned. He had his own Eiffel Tower, his own Mona Lisa. He had Mont-St-Michel, and from postcards he took landscapes from all over the world. He had flowers, he had stars. He had everything really.

His neighbours were amazed at the way he would work through the most extreme conditions at every spare moment of the day and often much of the night. Though some of the later bits look like clumsy sketches compared with the meticulous earlier work, he declared (at a time when he estimated he had put 29,000 hours into his work) that it was nearly finished. Not long afterwards in 1964 he dropped dead from exhaustion.

In Raymond Isidore's garden and house there are bits as beautiful as Matisse, as joyous as Klee or Dufy. It is like Smart's Jubilate Agno, like Blake, like the Douanier Rousseau. It is like Gaudi, it is like St Basil's Cathedral in Moscow. It is like nothing else. It makes the heart leap with joy. It is the distilled quintessence of happiness. It's wonderful, full of wonders and to be wondered at. It is a wonder of the modern world.

Most of Colin Ward's excellent book on Chartres is about the cathedral, but at the end he turns to Picassiette's house and says that its message (and the same could be said of Cheval) "is the one a whole stream of moral philosophers of art, John Ruskin, William Morris, Eric Gill, have drawn from the wonderfully sensitive and sophisticated but totally unknown creators of the cathedral. The artist is not a special kind of person. Every person is, or could be, a special kind of artist."

This article first appeared in the Guardian *on 19th August, 1995.*

OUT IN THE MID-DAY SUN

Some 20 years ago Les Powles gave up his job as a radio engineer and built himself a boat on which he has lived ever since. Not only that, he sailed single-handedly round the world in it. Then he did it again, in the other direction. Now, at the age of 70, he has stepped ashore at Lymington, Hampshire, having (not entirely deliberately) sailed from New Zealand to England non-stop. In spite of a capsize, he has lived for months often on no more than a slice of corn beef and a few spoonfuls of rice a day. This sounds like an improvement on his diet during the previous voyage, when he subsisted on rice mixed with toothpaste. Now, having lost five stone, he wants to put on a bit of weight and then sail to the Caribbean.

Why does he do it? Many people wouldn't even ask such a question. They're the ones who find nothing odd in the reply Mallory made when asked why he wanted to climb Everest: "Because it is there". To me this remark is simply daft. You might as well say you want to eat a cowpat "because it is there". And why do I very much *not* want to climb Everest? Because it is there.

Reaction to Mr Powles's latest exploit has generally concentrated on the survival aspect, which is indeed astonishing. But for a sedentary landlubber such as myself, what is remarkable is not that he finished the journey but that he should ever have wanted to start it. My own attitude is that of the Old English poem, "The Seafarer". "On dry land man loveliest liveth."

What is eccentric to one person is normal to another, and vice versa. When Mr Powles arrived in England, he was offered a bed for the night. He declined, preferring to sleep on his boat. To me that is as eccentric as anything else he has done. After six months, his sleeping conditions must have been terrible, but then I like clean sheets. Perhaps Mr Powles doesn't. A poet called William Wilkie accepted from Lady Lauderdale an invitation to stay the night on the condition that he was given a pair of dirty sheets. Wilkie detested clean sheets. He liked blankets, though, and slept under 24 every night.

There must by many people who, in the privacy of their own homes, do things that most of us would consider equally odd. The ones who hit the headlines usually do so through some public physical achievement like sailing round the world in a bathtub, or walking backwards from John O'Groats to Land's End. This is all acceptable unless it endangers the lives of people who have to rescue them, which the intrepid Mr Powles has not done.

Fortunately our society still abounds in eccentrics all over the place. They are an essential defence against conformity. What Tabasco sauce is to food, eccentrics are to society. Some of them you may find entertaining, some irritating, but we would be poorer without such characters as Eddie the Eagle, Spike Milligan, Dame Barbara Cartland, Patrick Moore, Magnus Pyke, Barbara Woodhouse and Sister Wendy Beckett. I confess that there are some in that list I can't abide.

And at a time when we have two political parties of scarcely distinguishable dullness, thank goodness for Ken Livingstone, Tony Benn and Tam Dalyell, and even for that matter Teresa Gorman and James Goldsmith, and the Yogic flyers of the Natural Law Party, Screaming Lord Sutch and Miss Whiplash.

Fine distinctions may have to be made between eccentrics, non-conformists and mavericks (named after Samuel A. Maverick, a Texas rancher who did not brand his cattle) and those people who are just dotty or neurotic. Some of these people can be a real pain, but I would suggest that an eccentric is someone who walks by himself without demanding company and is a law unto himself without wishing to impose that law on other people. The eccentric may be aware that his or her behaviour is different from that of most people, but still considers that behaviour to be most sensible. Being in a minority of one makes no difference.

Such unconventionality should at the very least be tolerated. In politics, arts and science it should be admired. J.S. Mill says, in *On Liberty:* "Eccentricity has always abounded when and where strength of character has abounded, and the amount of eccentricity in a society has generally been proportional to the amount of genius, mental vigour, and moral courage which it contained."

Eccentricity is an individual declaration of independence. Thoreau said that if a man isn't in step with his companions, "perhaps it is because he hears a different drummer. Let him step to the music he hears, however measured or far away."

Dr David Weeks is a clinical neuropsychologist at the Royal Edinburgh Hospital who has spent 10 years studying 1,000 eccentrics. He found that characteristics they have in common include bad spelling, non-conformity, creativity, curiosity, idealism, a happy obsession with one or more hobbyhorses (often five or six), intelligence, a mischievous sense of humour, unusual eating habits or living arrangements, and better than average mental and physical health.

Also, they live longer than most. Sounds all right. Of course, if everyone was eccentric, it would be eccentric not to be.

Guardian, *9th July, 1996.*

JOBS FOR THE BOYS

They were not long, the days of dons and poseurs. When the bright young aesthetes of the Brideshead generation left the privileged dissipation of their ancient universities they were — unless they had private means — faced with a real problem. Their expensive education had successfully taught them how to be affected snobs, but it had done precious little by way of equipping them to make a living.

It was not so bad for the Cambridge man. All he had to do was drink some sherry with the Senior Tutor who would put him in touch with the KGB which would fix up a young graduate with an interesting job in journalism or the Foreign Office or art history. For the Oxford chap it was more difficult. He not only lacked an introduction to the Kremlin but his options were further limited by his fastidious disdain for anything that smacked of trade or commerce. It is true that Anthony Powell went into publishing (a gentleman's profession in those days), and Henry Green into his family business of food engineers (of which he became managing director), but these were very much exceptions among the literary folk. More typical was John Betjeman, who resolutely resisted parental pressure to join the family firm making household gadgets. How, he asked, could he talk about samples and invoices and stock, and travel by tram to the Pentonville Road while wearing a Savile Row suit and a Charvet tie? You can see the problem.

One way of earning a living that was not utterly infra dig was to go back and teach in the very preparatory schools which they had themselves detested so much as pupils. Among those who chose to earn a crust by returning to the classroom were John Betjeman, Graham Greene, Evelyn Waugh, W.H. Auden, C. Day Lewis, Rex Warner, Christopher Isherwood, Geoffrey Grigson, John

Cowper Powys, James Hilton, Tom Driberg, T.H. White, Edward Upward, the future Nobel laureates T.S.Eliot and Samuel Beckett and countless others who were later to make their names with pen and paper rather than chalk and blackboard.

The usual staging-post on the way back unwillingly to school was through the offices of Messrs. Gabbitas and Thring's educational agency. Auden says in his letter to Lord Byron that

> The only thing you never turned your hand to
> Was teaching at a boarding school.
> Today it's a profession that seems grand to
> Those whose alternative's an office stool;
> To many an unknown genius postmen bring
> Typed notices from Rabbitarse and String.

In 1927 Cyril Connolly, planning a novel to be called *Green Endings,* thought that the waiting-room of Gabbitas and Thring would be a good subject for a "cynically dreary introduction."

In that waiting-room the seeker of employment first filled in a form giving full name, age, height, religion, school, university qualifications, lowest salary required (residential or non-residential), previous experience, games, and (even well into this century) a Yes/No as to intentions about going into Holy Orders.

Next came the interview. The would-be teacher talked to a member of the staff who then marked on the card his assessment of the applicant. Some of these comments are written in code. John Murrell (Managing Governor of the firm when I explored the archives a few years ago) explained the origins and workings of the code.

In the firm's early days they found a teaching job for a man whose name is now forgotten. Let's call him Mr Chalk. One day Mr Chalk looked out of his upstairs window and spotted the Head Master below him. For what doubtless seemed a good idea at the time Mr Chalk took the opportunity to empty his chamber-pot over the head of the Head. Not surprisingly he was sacked.

He was probably cracked as well, because he had the nerve to turn up at Gabbitas and Thring looking for a new job. The Gabbitas interviewer looked at the man's card, which by now contained a record of the piss-pot incident, and was understandably not too keen on recommending Mr Chalk for another job. Chalky then fell into a rage, seized the card, read it and stormed off to issue a libel writ.

After this incident the firm devised the code of the cards. Thereafter all applicants were described only in complimentary terms. Unless you were a complete rotter you were a Gent, but some Gents were more Gentlemanly than others. The top rank was Thorough Gent. One up on Gent was Gent MA, which did not mean a Master of Arts but a Gent in manner and appearance. The next category is Gent M, which is all right, followed by Gent A (which would be Captain Grimes). Good MA means that he is not a Gent, and at the very bottom of the heap is Fair M and A, which means that he's not to be touched with a bargepole.

When John Murrell joined the firm he looked up his own card and was a little miffed to find that he was not a Thorough Gent but a Gent MA. I was also a little miffed to find that (having myself gone through the process after Cambridge) there was no card at all for me in the files. Perhaps I was Fair M and A, and John Murrell (nearly a Thorough Gent) decided to spare my feelings or prevent a libel writ by removing my card. Fortunately the cards of some more distinguished applicants have survived* and as well as the coded descriptions there are thumbnail word-portraits *en clair*.

There's H.G.Wells, for example. Height 5 foot 7, with a slight knowledge of football, a weak chest, and offering to teach geology, zoology and drawing, but no music. If a music teacher was what you were after you would do

---
*1997; I understand they have since disappeared,

better with Ralph Vaughan Williams. Or how about learning violin, piano, organ and harmonium from Edward Elgar (who was at the time living on two bags of nuts a day: that information is from his biography, not the Gabbitas card).

Herbert Henley Henson's card shows him to be uncertain about his intentions as to taking Holy Orders, confessing to "doubts and questionings." He evidently overcame these, since he was ordained in 1885 and went on to become a Bishop of Durham every bit as controversial as a more recent incumbent of that diocese, the Rev. David Jenkins. Another interviewee who later became a bishop was described on his card as "An anaemic but promising-looking youth, who knows a great deal."

Or how about having a poet on your staff of teachers? Flecker, for example. He would have made a great Geography teacher, full of helpful advice as to the best route to Samarkand. Or, a few years later, Wystan Hugh Auden, height 5 foot 11, "quite a nice lad", offering to teach English, chemistry, biology, German and French. The Gabbitas and Thring commentary says rather cryptically "Reads. Modern in outlook." ("Reads, eh, Mr Thring?" "I'm afraid so, Mr Gabbitas." "Don't like the sound of that, Mr Thring. What's his bowling like?" "Modern, Mr Gabbitas, in outlook.")

C.S. Lewis refused to write John Betjeman a testimonial on the grounds that he could not say anything in his former pupil's favour except that he was "kind-hearted and cheerful." G. and T. more helpfully introduced Betch to three schools. All turned him down, but there was a firm offer of a job in Poland for 7,600 zlotys a year (about £176). The cards show him ending up less adventurously at Heddon Court from 1929-30.

Brendan Bracken was a notorious liar. In 1921 he gave his age as 22, "But see letter", G. and T. carefully note. *The Dictionary of National Biography* has him down as born 1901 in Tipperary; absconded from Jesuit College, Mungret; sent to Australia, 1916; settled in England,

1919; when aged nineteen he pretended to be sixteen and sent himself to Sedbergh until his money ran out after two terms, when he became a preparatory school teacher. By 1929 he was a Conservative MP, and among other things went on to found *History Today* and become chairman of the *Financial Times*. He was Churchill's parliamentary private secretary and throughout the war his chief crony, wielding considerable power and influence. In the war he was Minister of Information — just the job for someone who could tell such whoppers to Messrs Gabbitas and Thring. Not, I think, a Gent though he became a Viscount.

G. and T. seem to have spotted Bracken's false information about his age. What is strange is that he also claimed to them that he was currently teaching at Rottingdean School, Sussex. He *was* teaching at a preparatory school at the time but not Rottingdean. Some years later I was myself a pupil at that school and I have inherited from the headmaster (the late J.E. Maxwell-Hyslop) a complete set of the school magazine. Though it lists the staff every term there is no mention of Bracken at that or any other time.

In 1926 an enterprising 23-year-old came to G. and T. offering to teach drawing, painting and needlework, economics, Latin, French, English, History, Mathematics and all sorts of other things. Would she work in the Colonies or abroad (nice distinction here)? Yes, she would, and she could type 45 words a minute and take Shorthand at 100. For games she offered Physical Exercise. She wanted a salary of £80 if the job was residential, £150 non-residential. As it turned out, her achievements were not to be in teaching needlework. Instead she became the most celebrated aviatrix of all time, flying solo to Australia, making record-breaking flights all over the world, and finally perishing while ferrying planes for Air Transport Auxiliary in the Second World War. Her name was Amy Johnson.

And there's 5 foot 6 Madeleine Carroll who went on to be handcuffed to Robert Donat in *The Thirty-Nine Steps*, giving Hitchcock an opportunity to display her stocking-tops in a way which made an enduring impression on a whole male generation.

And so on, through Barnes Wallis (applying to teach maths in Switzerland) to Gilbert Harding (Gent M and A and good presence. No games, bad leg. Religion R.C. but not strict), Jimmy Edwards and (of course) Geoffrey Willans who went on to write the classic *Down With Skool!*

Gilbert Harding may have had no games, but what about Gilbert Jessop? He had "No Greek" and the card risks libel with "a rough diamond." He was also a Cricket Blue. Whatever Jessop's performance in the classroom may have been he played for Gloucestershire for 19 years, 13 of them as Captain, played in 18 Test matches, and played five innings of over 200; in 1903 he scored 286 in 175 minutes, and six of his 53 centuries were scored in less than an hour.

Evelyn Arthur St John Waugh, height 5 foot 7, offered as his subjects History, Eng Lit, Latin, Maths and Drawing. No games. A note on Waugh's card from the Headmaster of a school at Aston Clinton says that Waugh has been "worse for drink twice in four weeks." A Dr Crawford later provided information for a note that reads "Sacked. Came home drunk. Admits it." Christopher Sykes says in his biography of Waugh that "Then and afterwards Evelyn was unclear in his mind as to what offence he had committed." It sounds pretty clear.

William Joyce was a "Gent with an Irish accent, aged 36 (claiming to be 33)", 5 foot 6 and a half, offering to teach shooting, boxing and drill tactics, phonetics and languages. Later he became better known under the name of Lord Haw-Haw. Across his Gabbitas and Thring card is written in block capitals the one word HANGED.

The archives also contain information about the schools of the end of the 19th and beginning of the 20th century. Hornbrook House, Chislehurst, for example, offers "Dry gravel soil and is 300 foot above sea level." Oakfield, Haywards Heath, is on sand and gravel, is also 300 foot above sea level, but that is not all. It has "a very strong staff, including Non-Commissioned Officer for Drill and Gymnastics." One can just imagine this unusually strong staff. Classics would be taught by Geoff Capes, English by Mike Tyson, Divinity by Paul Gascoigne, mathematics by Arnold Schwarzenegger, history by Sylvester Stallone. Or you could send your son and heir to Quernmore House, Bromley, Kent, which goes one better than Hornbrook House by having "Unusually strong staff including Governesses."

There are certain pairs of names that seem to have a natural rhythm to them. Gilbert and Sullivan just sounds right; Sullivan and Gilbert could never have got off the ground, any more than such double acts as Jonathan and David, Hare and Burke, Wise and Morecombe, Spencer and Marks, Blackwell and Crosse, Decker and Black, Perrin and Lea, Hardy and Laurel, Mason and Fortnum, Jerry and Tom, let alone Hedges and Benson or Windus and Chatto or Circumstance and Pomp. So is it with Gabbitas and Thring.

They are unusual names. The most recent London telephone directory I can lay my hands on lists six Thrings and only three answering to the name of Gabbitas. Nearly a hundred years ago (and long before Auden) the firm was jocularly called Rabbitguts and String. Not everyone has found it easy to get their names right. The firm's archives include a file marked "Strange Envelopes." Strange indeed. Over the years the Post Office has managed to deliver to them letters addressed to, among others,

>Gaddi Talthring
>Mr Gabbitas et Shrinks,
>Mrs Gabitas and Thring
>Messrs Gabbitas Threng
>Coabettas, Thung Ltd
>Jaccobias Thring and Co.
>Grabbitas Ltd, Tring, Herts
>Jobbling and Thong
>Sir Gabbitas Thring

Gobbitas-Thorny
Sabbits, Strung and Co
Garrison and String
Respectable Gabbitas and Thing
The Gabbitas Hiring Company Ltd
Galbietras Shrey Co Ltd
Mr Gamts Thut
Gabbits' Ring Services
Gabbitas Thrivy
Gabits and Tidy.

And one letter was successfully delivered although it bore no stamp, no town, no street or number. All that was written on the envelope was Gabbitas and Thring.

The firm was founded in 1873 by Mr Francis Askin who took on John Gabbitas. For a while they were Askin, Gabbitas and Killick which as names go has a certain swing to it but Gabbitas was a man of vision and could see that there was room for improvement. Out went Askin and Killick, and in came Thring. Simple as that — Gabbitas and Thring.

The rightness of their names was about all that held them together, for Mr Gabbitas and Mr Thring were rarely on speaking terms. Thring wore a monocle and Gabbitas would refer to him as "That man upstairs who wears a damned piece of plate glass stuck in his blasted chops." Gabbitas was a snappy dresser, reckoned to be one of the best dressed men in London, and the bills for his tailors and bootmakers were steep. Thring once proudly told Gabbitas that his new trousers had cost him only half a guinea. Gabbitas replied that that's what they looked like.

Charles Thring's educational background was impeccable. His father was Dr Thring, who was to Uppingham what Dr Arnold was to Rugby. In his spare time he wrote hymns including "Fierce Raged The Tempest O'er The Deep." Gabbitas's origins were more obscure, and he discouraged inquiries into his private life. In his retirement he wrote a letter to the firm on the occasion of its fiftieth anniversary: in a postscript he says that "the less you say about me the better."

It is hard not to get the impression that Gabby was a bit of a rascal. He claimed to have been at the City of London school but their records provide no supporting evidence. And where did all his money come from? He had an expensive wardrobe and collected pictures, china and silver on a big scale. When he retired in 1904 Christie's sold some of his stuff for £80,000, which in modern terms must be quite a few million. A rock-crystal drinking vessel went for 15,500 guineas, the purchaser being Pierpont Morgan. When he joined the firm he was virtually penniless, his one asset being his abilities. It is hard to see how in the next 30 years he could have amassed quite such wealth.

He was an irascible man and could be extremely rude. He actually enjoyed having rows. After one had been blazing for an hour or so he would say "Let's get down to work," or "Let's go and have some lunch" and the row would be over. He had two passionate hatreds. One was the telephone. The other was women teachers. This resulted in a policy which effectively halved the firm's potential market. So with Gabbitas's full approval a Mr Truman left the firm and in 1901 opened an Agency for Governesses. Mr Truman was joined by Mr Knightely (also from G. and T.) and another double act was born — Truman and Knightely. As for the old firm, it is now called Gabbitas Educational Consultants Ltd. Poor Thring.

Guardian, *20th January, 1990*

PAUL, EMILE AND AIX

It's never fun being a new boy. Emile was thirteen when he went to the College Bourbon in Aix-en-Provence, and in the society of that small, oppressively enclosed town he was an outsider. His father, who had died four years earlier, was Italian: Emile himself did not become a French citizen until he was 21. His mother (now widowed and impoverished) came from the north of France, where Emile had spent his first years. At the College, the posh Provençal boys called him the *franciot* (Frenchy) because of his Parisian accent. He also had a slight lisp. He wasn't big, but he was bright and something of a swot. All in all he was prime bully-fodder. They sent him to Coventry.

There was a slightly older and tougher kid called Paul, also an outsider. He too was of Italian extraction, and he had been born out of wedlock. He did not come from one of the ancient bourgeois or aristocratic families that made up the stuffy arch-conservative Aix society. His father was a tough rough self-made man who had worked his way up from making hats to founding the first bank in Aix. He had bought the 45-acre estate of the Jas de Bouffan which in Louis XIV's time had belonged to the Marquis de Villars, the governor of Provence. In the eyes of that society he was worse than poor, as Emile's family was; he was nouveau riche.

Neither as a schoolboy nor at any other time in his life did Paul go out of his way to make himself popular. He broke the Coventry ban, chatted with Emile, got into a fight and was beaten up for his pains. The next day Emile thanked Paul by going to his home with a present of a basket of apples. Paul was Cézanne and Emile was Zola.

The population of Aix-en-Provence in the 19th century was only about 25,000. For its grammar-school to have produced two major historical figures is less probable than lightning striking in the same place twice (the grammar school at Stratford-upon-Avon only produced one). Not only that but it produced two simultaneously. What makes it still more extraordinary is that theirs was a friendship of exceptional intensity. Books on Zola refer to his schoolboy friend Cézanne, and books on Cézanne refer to his schoolboy friend Zola, as though each was a footnote in the life of the other. There was much more to it than that. To find such a close friendship among world-famous names you have to go back a long way and to the semi-legendary — Roland and Oliver, David and Jonathan — and the relationship between Zola and Cézanne (albeit with reversals) was life-long.

Baptistin Baille is a name that would not be remembered today if he hadn't been the third of the "three inseparables", though his role was always a Ringo-ish one subordinant to Zola and Cézanne. The three of them would go for long walks in the countryside around Aix; they would picnic; they would swim in the little river Arc. It was an Arcadian existence, an ideal of happiness. At the beginning of *L'Assommoir* there is a description of the hellish Paris laundry where Gervaise labours, and there she remembers being a laundress in Plassans (Zola's fictional name for Aix): "We used to take the washing to the river (Arc). It smelt better than it does here. It was a lovely place, a spot under the trees, with clear, running water."

Gervaise's memories echo the nineteen-year-old Cézanne's earliest known letter to Zola, written from Aix to Paris. "Do you remember the pine-tree which, planted on the bank of the Arc, bowed its shaggy head above the steep slope?" and the letter is accompanied with a drawing of the three young men swimming. In an autobiographical section of *L'Oeuvre* Zola writes that "They would spend whole days, stark naked, lying on the burning sand, then diving back into the water... They practically lived in the water and sunshine seemed to prolong their childhood..."

Both for Cézanne and Zola the memory of those days was a touchstone of happiness (as it was for poor Gervaise). It was always a reminder — that life could be like this; life should be like this. Zola tried to recreate it in his riverside house outside Paris at Medan. Cézanne tried to recreate it in his late pictures of bathers (with the addition of over-size female nudes, the sheer clumsiness of whom is as much psychological as pictorial).

As well as swimming and picnicking they read voraciously, mostly Victor Hugo and de Musset. They played music — Zola on clarinet, Cézanne on cornet. They serenaded one girl with these instruments until her parents emptied water jugs on them from an upstairs window. They thought a lot about girls. They also planned their careers, and their ambitions were Napoleonic. Zola always spoke of "conquering" Paris. Cézanne would "astound Paris with an apple". But first they had to get there.

Those of us from northern Europe or its offshore islands tend to see the South, the Midi, Provence, as a place of freedom and enlightenment. We think of Keats's beaker full of the warm South, or of van Gogh almost blinded by the yellow light and sunflowers of Arles. For Zola and Cézanne, on the other hand, the South was a place to get out of. Paris was where it was at. But the first thing to get out of was school. They were bright boys. One of them tended to win the writing prizes, the other the ones for drawing. That's right — Cézanne excelled in writing, Zola in drawing.

Both, though, had problems passing their *bac*, the matriculation exam. When Cézanne finally passed, his father made him study law, which he loathed as much as he later hated working in his father's bank. By then Zola had gone to Paris on his own (his penniless mother followed later) and found himself a new boy once more. At the Paris Lycée he was teased all over again, this time for being Provençal. His nickname (very funny, very cruel) was Gorgonzola. He had no money, he was alone, he was ill, he was unhappy. He longed for Aix and his friends. One summer holiday in Aix interrupts the flow of letters begging Cézanne to come to Paris so that they can achieve their ambitions. Emile tells of a dream in which he has written a book which Cézanne has illustrated. In the dream "Our two names shone together in gold letters on the title page and, in this brotherhood of genius, went inseparably on to posterity."

In his lifetime Cézanne was often referred to as the painter from Aix. Nowadays his huge reputation is based mostly on the pictures he painted in his studio in Aix or in the surrounding landscape, notably the Montagne Sainte-Victoire. From the almost inept tumult of his early paintings he worked to and achieved such classic calm that you might imagine him serenely contemplating the landscape of Provence and hardly ever budging from it. In fact Cézanne was never serene; he was always turbulent and restless. After his first visit to Paris in 1861 there was hardly a year in which half of it was not spent in Paris or its neighbourhood, and in the 1870s there are nearly four continuous years spent in the north. Even in his last years he took long trips from Aix. As far as I know he never painted a picture in or of Aix itself. His studios were always outside the town, as were his motifs. (There is a drawing that shows the tower of the Cathedral, seen from the studio above the town: the town itself is not indicated).

And yet wherever he went he took Aix and Provence with him (not least in the form of large quantities of olive oil). Provence was wherever he happened to be at the time. There are paintings done in Chantilly near Paris that could have been painted in the Aix family home, the Jas de Bouffan. The contrary is not the case.

Likewise there is a sense in which Zola also didn't leave Aix — the sense in which exiles never leave home (and he too had olive oil sent him whenever possible). He made a few visits South for necessary reasons such as burying his mother next to his father in the Aix cemetery, and to avoid the Franco-Prussian war and its aftermath. Otherwise he lived in the north but the whole of his great literary endeavour grows out of Aix. The massive twenty-volume series of novels begins and ends in Aix (Plassans). The best-known novels (such as *L'Assommoir, Nana, Germinal, La Bête humaine*) are set in the north, but the protagonists are all members of the Rougon-Macquart family which comes from Plassans. Even those like Nana who are born in Paris are twigs and branches on a family tree whose trunk and roots are firmly in Aix.

When Zola went to Paris he maintained contact with his friends in Aix through letters. Then Cézanne joined Zola in Paris to study art, and introduced to Zola the painters later known as the Impressionists, whom Zola was the first to champion in print. Cézanne also introduced Zola to Alexandrine ("Coco") who became his wife, and when they married he was Zola's best man. Zola dedicated his first real book to Cézanne (and Baille). When Zola became rich and Cézanne's father had halved his allowance, Emile sent money to Paul and his mistress (later wife) and their son. And so on. It was a very close friendship indeed, right into middle age.

In his edition of Cézanne's letters John Rewald says that "It is certain that for a long time Emile Zola was the only one to guess his (Cézanne's) sorrow, to feel the drama of this nature so rich in gifts, so poor in inner calm, just as he was the only one whose friendship and indulgence was great enough to retain Cézanne's confidence for more than thirty years." But the relationship was changing. Zola was no longer the one who was protected. He was very famous and very rich, whereas Cézanne was a failure not only in the eyes of the world but also (it becomes increasingly apparent) of Zola. His initial enthusiasm and proselytising for the Impressionists turned to disappointment and rejection.

Then in 1886, when the old friends were in their late forties, Zola published *L'Oeuvre*. Much of the novel is autobiographical, especially the early part in which the painter Claude is clearly Cézanne (as Sandoz is Zola). But in Zola's fictional framework Claude is also a Lantier, and the rules of Zola's novels dictate that any member of the Lantier family is as doomed as a member of the House of

Atreus or the protagonist of a Hardy novel. Sure enough, Claude is a failure in every way and hangs himself in front of his unfinished masterpiece.

Not for the first time a Zola novel proved explosive, and so it has been taken to be in the relations between the writer and his oldest friend. There are various points to bear in mind, however. Claude is not 100 per cent Cézanne; he is a composite figure. Not only Cézanne but all the other Impressionists objected to the book. Monet wrote a dignified letter of protest, the waspish Degas objected, and so did even that good and good-natured man Pissarro. Furthermore at this time Cézanne was going through a crisis which was either close to or actually a nervous breakdown. His father died and he had suddenly become not just independent but wealthy (I can't find any evidence that he ever re-paid the countless loans Zola had made him). He quarrelled not only with Zola but with practically everyone else. Pissarro thought he was going mad. The reasons for Cézanne's reaction to *L'Oeuvre* are thus more complicated than is usually made out but the upshot was that Cézanne acknowledged receipt of his complimentary copy from Zola and there is no record that they ever communicated again. Cézanne would have nothing to do with his old friend, while Zola (who was a kind man) always inquired of mutual friends and acquaintances visiting Aix as to how Paul was getting on.

Well, perhaps it's the weather, but people in Provence are very quarrelsome. (Pagnol, so sunny in his work, in life quarrelled with *everyone* from Raimu to Jean Giono.) On the Dreyfus case Zola and Cézanne were predictably on opposing sides. There were occasions when they could have met, but Cézanne wouldn't have it. But there was one thing they never disagreed about and that was their home town. "Wonderful place, vile people," Zola said of Aix repeatedly in one form or another. Cézanne felt the same. Emile Bernard records him saying that his compatriots were clods and that he despised them all: "At this point a look of indescribable contempt came over Cézanne's face and he shook his fist at the town of Aix."

Cézanne hated the weather in Aix. His letters rarely fail to mention that the weather is intolerably hot or intolerably cold. From early years children in the street had laughed at his unkempt appearance, to such an extent that they drove him to declare his firm intention of getting his hair cut. In his last years, diabetic and sometimes suffering from vertigo, his stumbling walk was taken for drunkenness and stones were thrown at him. An exhibition of his paintings in Marseille had to be closed because it was in danger of causing a riot. The director of the local museum, the Musée Granet, declared that while he was alive no painting by Cézanne would hang there: the man lived till 1921 and he kept his word. At present there are six paintings by Cézanne in the Musée Granet, all on loan from the Musée d'Orsay in Paris. Aix's treatment of Cézanne was shameful.

Zola's reasons for hating the Aixois went beyond being bullied at school. His Venetian father was an adventurer who was also a brilliant engineer in an age of such great French engineers as Gustave Eiffel. He was responsible for the conception and creation of the dam above Aix. The town had been notoriously dirty, unhealthy (with appalling cholera epidemics) and hot. The water from the Zola dam changed it into a town with clean drinking water and the countless fountains which make it so delightful today; Cocteau said that a blind man in Aix would think that the sun was always shining and that it was always raining.

François Zola died of pneumonia before the dam was finished. The company went bust, and the Zola family was left with nothing. The inexperienced young widow was probably diddled. The small Zola family suffered hardship but Emile's abiding grievance was not on financial grounds. What he couldn't forget or forgive was the humiliation to which his mother was subjected. With equal bitterness he resented the lack of recognition given to his father by the town which had benefited so much from his work.

In Paris in 1868, when he was beginning to make a name for himself, Zola heard about a fairly trivial incident in Aix which provoked him into a polemic of a ferocity that anticipated his *J'Accuse* letter which sparked the Dreyfus affair. He denounced Aix as a town that was stingy, petty and small-minded. A ferocious quarrel broke out between Zola and the local paper, the *Memorial d'Aix*. He did not ask for financial compensation but recognition of his father's achievement. It was an outrage that the Zola Canal had been renamed the Aix Canal. There was not a single road or square in the town named after his father. Zola won. The Aix Canal became the Zola Canal again, and a new road on the outskirts of the town was named after François Zola.

The comments made in his polemic hit home in Aix, and the outrage against Zola was compounded not only by the Dreyfus case (arch-Conservative and anti-Semitic Aix naturally being against) but also in the whole tenor of the 20 volumes of the Rougon-Macquart series. Aix simply hated Zola. His English translator Vizetelly wrote in 1898 (four years before Zola's death) that the town of Tarascon had never forgiven Alphonse Daudet for his "Tartarin"; and in a like way M. Zola, "who doubtless counts more enemies than any other literary man of the period, has none bitterer than the worthy citizens of Aix. They cannot forget or forgive the rascally Rougon-Macquarts."

Zola died of asphyxiation on 29 September 1902 from a blocked stove-pipe (was it misadventure, manslaughter or murder?). He was buried in Montparnasse cemetery by an enormous crowd of friends and admirers, and the railwaymen and coalminers he had championed in his novels. Anatole France said that for a moment in history Zola had been the conscience of mankind. France was speaking on behalf of the Academie Française which had always rejected Zola's membership, an honour he shared with Molière and Balzac.

When Cézanne's housekeeper brought him news of Zola's death he shouted what can only be translated as "Fuck off, fuck off! Leave me alone!" and locked himself in his studio all day, inconsolable.

After Zola's death his collection of paintings was sold in March 1903. It included ten works by Cézanne, which fetched good prices. This indirectly provoked a vicious hate campaign against Cézanne. Henri Rochefort, a political enemy of Zola's, took the opportunity of writing about the sale to attack Zola beyond the grave. He denigrated the collection in intemperate terms, picking out the Cézannes for special attention.

By this time it was known in Aix that Cézanne was beginning to enjoy a certain reputation in Paris. With truly provincial hyper-sensitivity the Aixois interpreted this as a sophisticated metropolitan joke at their expense. Since it was obviously impossible to admire Cézanne's paintings, the Parisians were only pretending to do so in order to make fun of Aix.

Rochefort's attack was therefore music to their ears. Someone bought 300 copies of the article and under cover of night slipped them under the doors of anyone in Aix suspected of harbouring any sympathy for the painter. Cézanne received threats and anonymous letters. He was as good as told to leave town. He told his son in Paris that he found copies of the article under his door every day, as well as those he received by mail.

In 1906 a statue of Zola was unveiled in Aix in the presence of the Mayor, the widow Alexandrine Zola and (right at the back) Cézanne. The statue had been left unfinished by another old school-friend, Philippe Solari, who had died earlier that year. Mayor Cabassol, son of Louis-Auguste Cézanne's partner in the bank of Cézanne & Cabassol, talked about Zola's youth, and about the Jas de Bouffan, and how in 1858 Zola had left Cézanne — "since become the great modern painter we know."

The Mayor was followed by Numa Coste, another old schoolfriend, who remembered "the three inseparables" of those early days: "We were then at the dawn of life... We dreamed of the conquest of Paris... When Zola had preceded the group to Paris he sent his first literary efforts to his old friend Paul Cézanne, at the same time letting all of us share his hopes. We read these letters amidst the hills, in the shade of the oak-trees, as one reads communiqués of the beginning of a campaign."

By now the tears were pouring down Cézanne's cheeks. The old painter probably couldn't see much at all as his old friends Numa Coste and Alexandrine Zola embraced in front of the bust of Emile Zola made years before by Solari, another old friend who had gone.

Le Memorial d'Aix reported the event in six lines. This is more than it gave to Cézanne when he died later that same year. I have been unable to find any report at all of the death of Cézanne in the local paper.

In November 1911 there was another Zola inauguration. It was a different bust but also by Solari, and it was mounted on a pedestal designed by Maurice Baille, nephew of Baptistin. This time there was a riot. The anti-Dreyfusard Conservatives, especially the Royalists, were vehement in their objection to a Zola statue. The *Memorial d'Aix* said that nothing justified a bust of an author who had slandered and libelled the Aixois when people such as Vauvenargues, Mignet and Thiers had no monument in the city. The report emphasises that there was not one public figure there, not a Senator, a Councillor or a Mayor. It was outsiders *(étrangers)* who had imposed the monument on them.

Zola's widow and family were there, though, and the Rector of the Academy of Aix. At the moment when the bust was unveiled Royalist demonstrators greeted the bust with a deafening noise of whistling. Fighting broke out. The police charged and there was a general free-for-all. Mounted police were called in and then a whole company of the 61st regiment. Twelve members of the proto-fascist Action Française were arrested. Finally things calmed down enough for the inauguration to continue in the presence of what the *Memorial* dismisses as about 50 people (photographs of the scene show that there were far more).

For some years I tried from time to time to find the Zola statue in Aix. I knew where it was meant to be but all that was there was a telephone box. Only recently I discovered that during the war the statue was melted down, presumably to make guns for the Nazis. I then learned that some time after the war a new statue was put up. But where? The Tourist Office repeatedly denied knowledge of any such statue. Eventually persistence was rewarded. The statue is in the Park Jourdan, a pleasant place but in the unfrequented outskirts of the town, and in a corner, as near to hidden as a statue that size can be.

Towns all over France have streets and squares named after Zola. In Aix there's a Boulevard, but again it's on the outskirts and father and son have to share it — the Boulevard François et Emile Zola.

The *Green Michelin* on Provence has a section on literature. In the current edition there is room to mention Henri Bosco, Alphonse Daudet, Jean Giono, Marcel Pagnol and even Peter Mayle. But not Zola. The only mention Zola gets in the book is as "friend of Cézanne", and that's it. He is not even in the Index. But he is in the Pantheon along with Voltaire, Rousseau, Victor Hugo, Jean Jaurès and Jean Moulin. Cézanne is buried in Aix in sight of the Montagne Sainte-Victoire, and not far from Zola's mother and father.

Like Zola, Cézanne worked literally till he dropped. His wife was summoned by telegram but she had an appointment with her dressmaker and arrived at the death-bed too late. The son and widow emptied the studio of pictures as quickly as they could. It seems they thought the prices would soon drop. The widow got through her money gambling. The son, far from inheriting his grandfather's financial acumen, showed rare incompetence, and got through what was a substantial cash fortune even without what he fetched for the paintings, now beyond valuation.

In 1954 Cézanne's studio was on the point of demolition for redevelopment, an idea that was popular in Aix. Just in time it was acquired by the Cézanne scholar John Rewald and American admirers of Cézanne. They gave it to the University of Aix, which in turn gave it to the town. In very recent years Aix has began to make amends to Cézanne, and is even proud of him. Zola is viewed not so much with hostility as indifference. I recently met the Deputy Mayor in charge of cultural matters, Mme Germaine Pivasset. She was born in Aix and she told me that throughout her schooldays nobody ever mentioned that the town is the Plassans of Zola's novels. It would be extraordinary if someone was brought up in Dorchester without being aware that the town had some connection with Thomas Hardy, but that is how it is with Aix and Zola.

Guardian, *3rd February, 1996*

BUCKMINSTER ABBEY

By eight o'clock every seat was full in the Central Hall, Westminster (capacity 2,641), and many people had been turned away. The audience sat there patiently, their intellects waiting to give full attention to whatever message Buckminster Fuller had to impart. "Will he go on for long?" someone said in the row behind me, as though asking if an elephant would be big, or an octopus have many legs. A know-all voice replied "He'll have to stop by half past ten because the hall's only let till then."

By quarter past eight there was still no sign of Buckminster and I had become uncomfortably aware that I would probably not be able to last out until half past ten, or that if I did it would be at the expense of concentrating on not bursting rather on the speaker's words. The need for a pee had to be weighed against the embarrassment of making half the row (I was in the middle) stand up twice, and walking out and in before a watchful audience (I was also near the front of the hall). The pee won.

The foyer outside the hall was deserted. Everyone who was not sitting expectantly inside had been turned away. In the Gents there was only one other person, a little old man in a blue suit. He had very close-cropped white hair, and there was sticking plaster wrapped round the part of his glasses that holds onto the ears. As he was having his pee he stared ahead at the white glazed tiles in front of him with a blank, fixed expression.

I returned, much relieved, feeling that I would now be able to listen with undivided attention. The moment I opened the door of the hall, applause broke out, and as I walked down the aisle Michael Kustow introduced the speaker with commendable brevity. People had hitchhiked from as far as Glasgow to hear Bucky this evening, he said, and with an audience as keen as that there was no further need to introduce (wave of the hand) — *Bucky*.

By now I had reached very nearly the front of the hall and the dreadful thought occurred to me that, however improbable the idea, the audience might suppose that I, striding towards the stage throughout Kustow's introduction, was Bucky, the inventor of the geodesic dome and the Dymaxion House. This time, plunging headlong down the row, making everyone stand up once more and trampling on their feet, overcoats and handbags, far from being embarrassed, I felt embarrassment positively dropping away from me as I sank into the anonymity of being a mere member of the audience — my second relief in five minutes.

When I had settled back into the seat and recovered my cool I was able to attend to the figure on the stage, who had begun to talk. He looked even tinier up there than he had in the Gents. His trousers were too short, as the trousers of Americans often are. He moved somewhat stiffly, like a robot or a clockwork toy, at first speaking rather jerkily, not very loud and quite slowly. It was not his custom, he said, to prepare his lectures. He tried not to even think about what he was going to say beforehand: he believed in thinking out loud. When he was young, if someone went from his home town to New York, they would talk about it for days. His granddaughter, he went on, lives near Idlewild airport, Kennedy airport it's now called, and every time an aeroplane flies over, which is pretty often, someone says to her, "Look, there's an aeroplane," but she's never seen a bird in her life. And all the children's books are about cows and sheep and chickens which don't mean a thing to her and are so remote from her experience that children's stories might just as well be about polio viruses.

He had begun to talk a bit faster by now and, having moved the glass and pitcher of water, was perched on the table like a garden gnome. His feet nowhere near reached the ground. Everything we had been taught at school, it seemed, was all wrong. We were told that a triangle has 180 degrees, but that's a triangle on a plane and planes don't exist. We live on a sphere, where things are very different. If he drew a line from the North Pole, it would meet the Equator at a right angle. If he drew another line from the Pole at right angles to the first line it would also meet the equator at a right angle. There we were then, a triangle with three right angles, not 180 degrees at all, but 270.

We all sat up a bit at this, as though we had just witnessed a television newsreader produce three white rabbits out of his left ear. From this point Fuller (sorry, Bucky) went on to dazzle us with every trick in the lecturer's box. He instructed, he made us laugh, he harangued, he sometimes got angry with us, and he made us think, as he sprayed the audience with a machine-gun fire of facts and ideas. You can get eight cubes round a single point, but you can get 32 tetrahedrons (at the time this seemed very important, but I can't now remember why). He sketched a scenario of the discovery of the lever (pronounced to rhyme with "ever"). A man walking through a forest came to a spot where a lot of logs had fallen on top of one another. The man stepped on the end of one log, and as that end went down the other end lifted a log that weighed much more than the man. The man took the log home because he thought it had magical powers, and he used it for lifting other heavy objects. Then one day the man's wife said "You know, I think any log would do." (This, if I remember rightly, was an example of a first-degree generalisation). The audience laughed at the wife's remark, but the narrator looked as bleakly stern as ever, his mouth snapped shut like a bulldog clip.

He told us how difficult it was to explain how a gyroscope works without using a lot of mathematics, and then did so. As he talked of the various orbits through which a top can spin, he imitated them, spinning around the platform. He didn't spin at great speed, and at the age of 74 he lacked some of the grace of a ballet dancer, but it was a wonderful piece of mime. The frail little old man *became* a top, spinning first on a point, then (still spinning) moving round in a circle, then developing a wobble.

What about a gyroscope? Imagine someone throwing the hammer. The tiny old man transformed himself into a husky athlete as he seized the imaginary triangular handle and began to hurl the imaginary weight around him. When the athlete has got the weight going nicely, he said (stepping into another role), he asks him to fasten it to a strong belt he's wearing. He gives the athlete another hammer, and when this is going nicely another hammer, and another, until the belt is solid with hammers. Element by element the gyroscope was built up, and we learned why gyroscopes behave in such odd ways, why they right themselves, why they do the opposite of what you would expect. I couldn't explain it all now, but while he was talking I understood.

How many of us knew what "synergy" means? Would we please put our hands up? There was a small, pitifully small, show of hands. He looked severely down on us and reckoned that about 3 per cent knew what synergy meant. Synergy — again if I understood rightly — is the ability of a whole to behave in a way that could not be predicted from any prior knowledge of the individual parts.

Synergy was the only word that meant this, and the fact that only 3 per cent of us understood what the word meant showed that not many people were thinking about this important concept. He was extremely stern about this, and not at all pleased, and I decided to mend my ways and spend a great deal of time thinking about synergy in the future.

He also explained to us what precession means, about which a show of hands had shown us to be only slightly less shamefully ignorant. He demonstrated to us the difference between mind and brain. Before our very eyes, with no visual aids, he subjected an imaginary rope to such tension that he could hardly speak with the effort. He bundled together invisible steel rods, each in itself flexible, into a solid honeycomb pattern, and in doing so he transformed himself into the giant I had always imagined him to be from his photographs.

As the clock behind him ticked past ten, he consulted his watch more and more often. He spoke faster and faster, and the ideas came at us with accelerating and bewildering speed. We had to learn to *think*, he said, and struck the side of his head with a resounding smack that reminded us that the giant we had by now become accustomed to was the same tiny old man we had seen at the beginning of the lecture.

He explained the world to us, and it seemed that he could save the world too. All the problems could be solved by 1985. He didn't despise those who had gone before him, any more than he despised the umbilical cord he had been born with. But the umbilical cord had outlived its usefulness and could be thrown away. Certainly, it seemed, we should not suppose that he was just a John the Baptist.

It was the most breathtaking sermon I have ever heard. We were instructed in the scriptures, we were allowed a very brief glimpse of the promised land. Then, at 10.29, a blistering vision of hell fire. We had to start to think or (glance at watch) we would perish.

As the audience applauded he became a little old man again. He nodded his head at the audience, again a jerky clockwork toy. Nod, nod, nod, walk half way off the platform, nod, nod. Then, still without a smile, he was gone.

Everyone got up, collecting their coats, feeling shaken and making firm resolutions to try and do better in future. He had talked for two and a quarter hours, but on the way out I kept hearing people say that it was a pity he had had to stop: he had just got going.

This article first appeared in New Society *on 12th March, 1970. Richard Boston also interviewed Bucky a few days before he died in 1983. A copy of the interview is available from Five Leaves on request.*

THE GAME OF THE NAME

One of the least serious problems brought about by the population explosion is the world shortage of names. A recent Reuter report says that *China Youth News* has announced that China's 1.2 billion people are running out of names. Researchers at the Chinese Academy of Sciences suggested that China should create new surnames, revive out-of-date ones, borrow foreign surnames and adopt family names translated from minority languages.

This problem is not confined to China. Throughout the world people are making bold and brave efforts to cope with the problem. Look at the Clintons and the fine example they have set. Did Hillary and William Jefferson Clinton call their female infant Jean or Jane or Joan or June? They did not. They called her Chelsea. Likewise with Sir Bob Geldof and his ex-wife-to-be Paula Yates. One of their offspring is called Fifi Trixibelle. And why not? Because it's silly, that's why not.

Meanwhile in Panama the election tribunal has launched a campaign to persuade parents to be a bit more sensible in the choice of the names they give their newborn. This was after the census produced an embarrassing number of Panamanians with such names as Adolfo Hitler, Benito Mussolini, Alitalia, Chevrolet and Vagina.

In France, Monsieur Gérard Guillot is bringing a case before the European Court of Human Rights to allow him to give his daughter the forename of his choice. When she was born on April 7, 1983 he trundled down to the Town Hall of Neuilly-sur-Seine with the intention of registering her name as Fleur de Marie, after the heroine of a novel by the 19th-century popular novelist Eugène Sue. Gérard was met with blank refusal. He was told the laws of France only permitted the names of saints or characters from classical history. The result is that the French are impoverished in the forename department and have to do the best they can with such variations as Jean-Paul, Jean-Luc, Jean-Marie and Marie-Claire, Marie-Claude, Marie-Helène and Marie-France.

This outstandingly stupid law was changed in 1993, by which time the would-be Fleur de Marie was 10, and still legally nameless. Don't ask me why the case is still lumbering on, or what Madame Guillot thinks of it, or the daughter (who could, I suppose, be called Guillotine).

Recently in Sweden the parents of a five-year-old called Albin were fined 5,000 kronor because officialdom would not accept that while his name was pronounced Albin it was spelt Brfxxccmnpccccllllmmmnprxclmnckssqlbb-11116. The court rejected the parents' plea but conceded that it was "a pregnant, expressionistic development that we see as an artistic creation". For the life of me I can't see what's wrong with Brfxxccmnpccccllllmmmnprxclmnckssqlbb11116. The Finnish language is full of words that look like that. In fact I suspect that the decision of the Swedish court in the case of Brfxx...etc was an anti-Finnish one. The Swedes and the Finns have never got on.

What caught my eye about this story is that the Swedish town in which the Brfxx... family lived was Halmstad. While trying to escape the Swinging Sixties I fled to Sweden and spent a year there teaching English in this very town of Halmstad. Roughly half my girl pupils were called Christina or Ingrid and the boys were called Karl, Sven or Ingmar. As for surnames, Andersson, Johanson and Svenson were more common than Smith or Brown with us.

In my class in Halmstad there may well have been the parents of Brfxx...etc. They might even have been — good grief — the grandparents. I used to compare the lack of imagination of my pupils' names with such English glories as Rudyard and Makepeace and Shufflebottom and Cholmondeley. Can my light-hearted remarks have born fruit in Brfxxetc? Few teachers can claim such direct results from their time in front of the blackboard.

Sweden is a huge and beautiful country but it is much the same in one place as another. It consists of mountains and streams, which is why there are so many people called Bergström which means mountain stream, and Bergman, which is mountain-man. The efficient Swedes decided at the time I was there that it would be administratively easier if there weren't quite so many people going around with the same name. So they set up a quango with the task of thinking up new names and persuading the Svensons and Johansons to take less common ones. The girl I was in love with at the time was called Angela Ljungström (heather-stream) and she worked for this name-change quango. (By the way, Angela, it would be nice to hear from you c/o the *Guardian,* 119 Farringdon Road, London EC1, Storbritannien.) Could it be Angela who is responsible for Brfxxccmnpccccllllmmmmnprxclmnckssqlbb11116? I would like to think so.

Wales also has a major name problem, what with everyone being called Jones. The solution there is the soubriquet, like Jones the butcher or Jones the fish, or (hullo, Terry) Jones the Python. There was once an old Welshman who lost all his teeth except two. One was an upper tooth in the middle and the other survivor was a lower tooth in the middle. So he was called Jones Central Eating.

There is nothing new about this name-calling. In fact it was the first job given to the ancestor of us all. I refer you to the book of Genesis, chapter 2, verse 19. "And out of the ground the Lord God formed every beast of the field, and every fowl of the air; and brought them unto Adam to see what he would call them; and whatsoever Adam called them every living creature, that was the name thereof."

Think of old Adam there, in the Garden of Eden, all alone: Eve came later. What fun it must have been, going round saying you're called Giraffe, you're Greater Crested Grebe, you're Duck-Billed Platypus. Paradise.

The Game of the Name first appeared in the Guardian *on 23rd July, 1996.*

The Angela Ljungström mentioned also introduced me to the world of Charlie Brown (see page 160). By pure chance she saw the above article in far-off Stockholm and got in touch with me a year later. By another co-incidence that same week the Brfxxx... story (by now well over a year old) re-surfaced as new news in the Daily Telegraph, *which was followed by other newspapers, including the* Guardian.

THE YOUNG AVIATOR

Biggles is one of those fictional characters — like Bunter and Jeeves and Pinocchio and Sherlock Holmes, like Falstaff and Don Quixote for that matter — who are known far beyond the actual readership of the works they occur in, vast as that readership was, and still is. In 1964 the first UNESCO statistical handbook placed Biggles 29th on the list of the most translated books, and Biggles was rated the most popular juvenile hero in the world. Captain W.E. Johns's books were translated into nearly 20 languages and were made into comic strips, radio serials, television and cinema films. When he died in 1968 he had published 169 titles. Biggles accounted for 104 of these, and there were eleven Worrals (WAAFs), ten Gimlet books (Commandos), ten science fiction, five Steeley thrillers and an assortment of others including one on gardening (*The Passing Show:* a garden diary by An Amateur Gardener).

Who was Captain W.E. Johns? There is no such rank as Captain in the RAF, or in the Royal Flying Corps which preceded it. An Army Captain is a sufficiently low rank rarely to be retained in civilian life other than by instructors of physical training or racecourse officials. Captain Grimes in *Decline and Fall* is certainly not an ex-sea captain, and if Johns was a naval Captain how did he know so much about aeroplanes? In fact his rank was bogus. Johns rose to the rank of Flying Officer in the RAF, and it was as Flying Officer Johns that he wrote his first books. In 1932 he promoted himself to Captain, explaining with disarming frankness that he thought it sounded better.

Like ex-President Reagan and ex-Mr Jeffrey Archer, Johns had a problem distinguishing between fact and fiction. During the First World War his plane was shot down by Fokker DVIIs of Ernst Udet's Jagdstaffel, his gunner was killed and Johns spent the rest of the war as a POW.

Udet was an air ace in the same class as Manfred von Richthofen (known to Snoopy as the Red Baron). It was a good enough story but not enough for the fantasist Johns to have been shot down by Udet's squadron: it had to be by Udet personally. In 1960 he told the *Evening Standard* that after he crashed Udet landed nearby, "saluted my dead gunner, got me to a doctor in the village and said 'Bad luck. My turn tomorrow.'" Unfortunately for Johns, some rotter checked on this story and it turned out that Udet was on leave at the time. (Someone who really was around was Hauptmann Hermann Goering.)

Another Johns story tells how in the 1920s he was an RAF recruiting officer. "One day a thin, pale-faced chap walked in. There was something so off-hand about his manner, almost amounting to insolence, that I took an instinctive dislike to him. I had got to know the type. He was 'different' from the other recruits and he was letting me know. He gave his name as John Hume Ross." This was the man who became Aircraftsman Ross, no 352087, better known as T.E. Lawrence.

Ross had no credentials and Johns told him to get a birth certificate and three character references. Johns meanwhile checked with Somerset House and when Ross returned with faked documents challenged him. Ross admitted that Johns was right, and Johns kicked him out, only to have him return within an hour with an Air Ministry note, the signature on which persuaded Johns to do as he was told and admit the fraud to the Air Force. He sent Ross for a medical and the medical officer looked at Ross's scarred back and rejected him on physical grounds. Again the Air Ministry intervened and ignored Johns's protests. Such was Johns's story.

There doesn't seem to be any truth in it, other than details Johns could easily have acquired without personal knowledge. Well, George IV was convinced that he had been in command at the Battle of Waterloo, and Osbert Lancaster's father-in-law was so excited by Blériot's flying across the Channel that he came to think he had himself been in the cockpit with Blériot at the time.

Other stories Johns told about himself prove to be equally ill-founded, but his biggest confusion was between himself and Biggles. Speaking of his paragon he modestly said (*News Chronicle* 1938), as Flaubert did of Madame Bovary, "In a way he is myself."

So who was Biggles? We first meet him in *The Camels are Coming*. These camels are not cud-chewing artiodactyl mammals (that's P.C.Wren and Beau Geste, which I would have been reading at about the same time I first read the Biggles books) but aeroplanes, the celebrated Sopwith Camels (also of Snoopy fame). In the foreword Johns introduces his hero thus:

> Captain James Bigglesworth is a fictitious character, — with, as it happens, the same fictitious rank as his creator — yet he could have been found in any RFC mess during those great days of 1917 and 1918 when air combat had become the order of the day and air duelling was a fine art. "Biggles," as I have said, did not exist under that name, yet he represents the spirit of the RFC — daring and deadly when in the air, devil-may-care and debonair when on the ground.

He is also "fearless but modest, efficient and resolute" — a latter-day Chevalier Bayard in fact, *sans peur et sans reproche,* just like "Captain" Bill Johns.

In *Biggles Learns to Fly* our hero is "aged 17, slim, rather below average height, and delicate looking... his eyes... were what is usually called hazel." Usually, but not always. In *The Cruise of the Condor* they are grey. "His features were finely cut, but the squareness of his chin and thin line of his mouth revealed a certain doggedness... Only his hands were small and white, and might have been those of a girl."

Is he a dog? Is he a girl? The head spins, the blood runs cold. Just suppose that it turned out that in fact Biggles was *a girl*. All the time. It is unlikely, but was Biggles a homosexual? Strictly in the closet, of course. The evidence shows that he kept company almost entirely with men. His closest associates are Algy, Ginger and Bertie. Algy is an aristocrat and a confirmed bachelor, as Biggles is. Ginger Hebblethwaite on the other hand is working class, is described oddly as a "waif" and as Biggles's "protégé". It is perhaps worth pointing out that in rhyming slang a ginger is (via ginger beer) a queer, but there is good evidence that Ginger is straight since in *Biggles in the South Seas* he falls helplessly for a Polynesian female called Full Moon. The same book contains the sentence "Yes, it's a girl: I can see her talking to Smyth." Obviously there was nothing queer about Smyth.

Our next witness is Bertie Lissy. When we first meet him in *The Fledglings* he is playing the piano. This is a straw in the wind if ever there was one. He's playing Liszt, which is another straw in the wind. And it turns out that at flying school his nickname was Sissy and he is "a slight, almost effeminate youth on whose fair hair the setting sun gleamed like liquid gold." In *Biggles in the Orient* he is "effeminate in face and manner." All right, Captain, we've got the idea. He's a roarer.

Johns said in an interview that "Boys hate the introduction of girls into their stories." Certainly for most of the time Biggles and girls are poles apart — "Biggles shrugged his shoulders and looked at Ginger helplessly, for the female mentality was one of the things he did not understand" *(Biggles and Co)*. Yet in the same book —

> "A girl! by Jove! you're right. Good gracious, it's Stella Carstairs."
>
> Ginger threw Biggles a quick look.
>
> "I didn't know you two were on visiting terms," he remarked suspiciously.

At the end of Chapter 3 of *The Camels are Coming* we read: "'Get me a drink somebody, please,' he pleaded." The Perelmanesque "please, he pleaded" cannot disguise the fact that this is a drinking Biggles. The next chapter ends, "Never mind," said the Colonel soothingly, "you'll be able to get marvellously drunk tonight." "Me! Drunk!" said Biggles disgustedly, "I never drink whisky." What a casuist — on page 109 he's drinking rum.

One thing leads to another. First it's booze and the next thing you know it's girls. *In Affaire de Coeur* —

> "Are you looking for me, Monsieur?" said a voice which sounded to Biggles as musical as ice tinkling in a cocktail glass. Turning, he beheld a vision of blonde loveliness in blue silk, smiling at him.

Marie Janis's voice sounds to the near-dipsomaniac Biggles like ice tinkling in a cocktail glass. In the first sentence of Thurber's *The Secret Life of Walter Mitty* "The Commander's voice was like thin ice breaking." What is more, when Mitty is the intrepid aviator single-handedly taking on Von Richtman's circus he also holds the rank of Captain. Not the least of W.E. Johns's achievements was to provide the raw high-octane cliché material which parodists such as Thurber, Perelman and Glen Baxter have found such a rich vein of comedy.

But back to Marie Janis. Biggles immediately spots that this vision of blonde loveliness is not a chap. She just as swiftly spots his weakness for the bottle and offers him *un petite verre*. Her uncertain grasp of the French gender system should have tipped Biggles off, but no — he is drunk and in love and probably monoglot.

> "Marie," whispered Biggles, as their lips met. Then, his heart beating faster than Archie or enemy aircraft had ever caused it to beat (*Archie? What's he doing here?*) he suddenly

pushed her aside, rose to his feet and looked at the luminous dial of his watch. "Time I was getting back to quarters," he said unsteadily.

And none too soon, for the beautiful Marie turns out to be a German spy. Typical, really. Probably all girls are German spies deep down. Biggles has had a narrow escape and steers clear of them in future, but first he consoles himself in a big way with the bottle. The CO is soon informed that "Biggles is finished unless he takes a rest... He's drinking whisky for his breakfast, and you know what that means — he's going fast. He drank half a bottle of whisky yesterday morning before daylight, and he walked to the sheds as sober as I was."

Biggles gets pissed, crashes his plane, pulls himself together and thereafter (on strict publisher's orders) it's no booze and no birds for Biggles for the next half century. When the early books were re-issued in the 1950s the whisky was changed into lemonade, which made for some very curious reading.

As for sex, it was now segregation all the way, to such a thorough extent that the girls got their own books and their own heroine, Pilot Officer Joan Worralson of the WAAF. Readers of a Freudian inclination will not fail to notice that the abbreviation of her name to Worrals involves cutting off the son — roughly.

Worrals is aged 18, has dark hair and is intrepid. Her side-kick (with whom she co-habits) is Betty Lovell, known as "Frecks". Although Frecks is blonde and has a weakness for chocolates, she is if anything even more prudish than Worrals herself and is always on hand to interrupt at the slightest sign of what she calls sob-stuff. Spitfire pilot Flying Officer Bill Johns — I mean Bill Ashton — has obviously got the hots for Worrals from whom (just as obviously) he gets short shrift. On one particularly dangerous mission he manages a hand-hold. "Bill," says Worrals, "You're not by any chance making love to me, are you?... Be yourself. You'll laugh at this nonsense in the morning."

Worrals and Frecks are not just ball-breakers; they are man-eaters. "I'll shoot you," she says in *Worrals in the Wilds*. And she does. "I've killed far better men than you." And she has.

Worrals is a feminist. "Who started the war anyway? Men... Take a look at the world and see what a nice mess men have made of it." Biggles wisely steered clear of her. At any rate there is no record of their ever having met. Can this be because in fact *Worrals was Biggles in drag?* Or vice versa?

* * *

Johns wrote better than, say, Agatha Christie, but his work often shows signs of the haste with which such quantities of books can only have been produced. He repeats plots over and again and self-plagiarises endlessly. He gets details wrong. A hand-gun is referred to as a revolver and an automatic on the same page. A centipede is referred to as a reptile. He says infer when he means imply. None of this matters in view of the rich rewards of Johns at his unique best.

This comes in two forms. One is the Fine Writing. "The pink hue of dawn had turned to turquoise when Mahoney turned for home at the end of the dawn patrol." The purist may object to two turns and two dawns in one fairly short sentence, but it is as close to being a literally purple patch as you could hope for.

As a writer of prose Johns was a virtuoso of the "Somewhere a dog barked" School of Writing, (identified by Peter de Vries in, if I remember rightly, *Reuben, Reuben*). A brief riffle through the pages of Johns rewards us with: "Once, far away, an owl hooted mournfully, and something splashed furtively in the moat." (A questing vole, I would guess, in the plashy fen). "From somewhere out on the moor, distant but clear in the silence, came the sound of a dog barking furiously." *(Biggles and the Dark Intruder.)* A few pages later "From somewhere in front the

sound of voices came eerily through the clammy mists."
Then "Somewhere in the distance a car horn hooted."

Far better writers than Johns are much less quotable. Once you start it is hard to stop. Algy turned a trifle pale... Biggles threw him a curious smile... The girl's nostrils quivered... Page after page is the raw material of parody. "By heavens they've done us! It's stannic chloride. Watch out!" And then there's the rich repertoire of exclamations, from "Great Scotland Yard!" to "Stiffen the crows!", "Suffering rattlesnakes!" and "Jehoshaphat!"

But Johns's real mastery is in the comic-strip narration:

> Biggles was on its tail in a flash. Through his sights he saw it still climbing. Rat-tat-tat — he cursed luridly as he hammered at the gun which had jammed at the critical moment. The Fokker had Immellmanned and was coming back at him now, but Biggles was ready, and pulled his nose up to take it head on.

Johns isn't just quotable, he's memorable. "The Fokker had Immelmanned." I first read that more than 40 years ago and its poetry has not staled, probably because I still haven't a clue what it means.

Johns and Biggles have from time to time been denounced by librarians, who hate Enid Blyton, W.E. Johns and Richmal Crompton with an awesome passion. In 1963 St Pancras library removed all three from their shelves. In 1970 Ipswich's chief librarian banned Biggles for being "fascist". Librarians around that time accused the Biggles books of sexism, of the glamourising of violence and war, of racism, nationalism and imperialism. Peter Grosvenor in the *Daily Express* commented that "The extraordinary thing about children's books is that the more popular they are with children the less popular they are with librarians."

Johns answered his accusers on the violence issue when he told Geoffrey Trease in 1948 that "In more than 40 novels (Biggles) has only struck a man once, and that was a matter of life and death...." This is another of Johns's fibs. A few minutes' search comes up with "Biggles steadied his man with a left, then sent the right hard and true to the jaw. The man dropped without a sound, out to the wide" and "Acting with the speed of light, he brought his fist up with a vicious jab into the pit of the man's stomach. There was a choking grunt as the man collapsed."

That's two for starters, and in practice Biggles and his chums are forever upper-cutting, delivering straights to the jaw and causing people to measure their length on the ground (I still can't visualise this phrase without a tape-measure coming into it). Having said which, I did find on re-visiting Biggles after rather a long time that there really is less violence than I had expected, and Johns never shows the sadistic pleasure in behaving with extreme prejudice that characterises the unspeakable Sapper and Dornford Yates (also among my boyhood reading) and Ian Fleming.

What Johns did glorify was the aviator, quoting with approval Lloyd George's tribute to "The cavalry of the clouds... the knighthood of the air." But glorifying the warrior is not the same as glorifying the war. Johns had first-hand experience of battle in Gallipoli and Salonika as well as in the air. In 1938 he wrote in *Flying* magazine that war is "the crowning infamy of slavery of man to the master who, in his folly, he sets up over him." In *The Rescue Flight* he describes a young First World War pilot who is "shocked to realise that he did not really know what everybody was fighting for. Something about Belgium."

Far from being a Fascist beast Johns was consistently and persistently anti-Franco. In *Popular Flying* (March 1939) he wrote:

> I have an increasing suspicion that our so-called democracy is nothing like as democratic as it pretends to be. If it was — to take only one example — could it stand by unmoved

> and watch the cold-blooded murder of its friend in democracy — Spain? For do not be misled. The Spanish Government — by which I mean republican Spain — is as democratic as a government can be. It was elected by the vote of the people. That it was a Left Wing government makes not the slightest difference. It was the will of the people.

In *Biggles in Spain* "Ginger wondered what curious urge had induced the little cockney to abandon peace and security for a war, the result of which could make no possible difference to him. The same could be said of nearly all the other members of the International Brigade." Pure Orwell.

In the same book Johns takes a line that is almost explicitly pacifist: Jock McLannock is

> ...a wild Scotsman from Glasgow, a pilot of high social position who had abandoned his Highland home *(Eh? Glasgow in the Highlands?)* to fight in what he considered to be the cause of freedom and justice — a cause for which millions of men since the beginning of time have laid down their lives, usually in vain.

Again, in *Biggles of the Camel Squadron,* our hero reflects in his single-seater, "Around, above and below, was a scene of peace and unutterable loveliness. It was hard to believe that within a few miles thousands of men were entrenched, waiting for the dawn to leap at each other's throats. War! he was sick of it, weary of flying, and the incredible folly of fighting men that he did not know."

Johns was as opposed to the other dictators as he was to Franco. He was against appeasement in the 1930s and took a Churchillean line on rearmament: "It is my firm conviction that only by a fair balance of power can peace be maintained." This resolute position got him the sack from the editorship both of *Popular Flying* and the weekly magazine *Flying*.

To call Johns Fascist is to show no knowledge or understanding either of Johns or Fascism. Imperialist, certainly: "'No, chaps,' Biggles said, as they walked slowly towards the exit, 'it's just because any Britisher would do what we've done that the old Empire goes on.'"

The Empire, the crown and public schools: these are what Johns and Biggles stood for. He told Geoffrey Trease, "I teach a boy to be a man... I teach sportsmanship according to the British idea... decent behaviour... I teach the spirit of team-work, loyalty to the crown, the Empire and lawful authority." These are not Fascist values, and they are not the values of today, but they are pretty much the values inculcated in me at school from 1945 to 1956. And these values were simply not questioned. It is extraordinary to me now that an intelligent and decent man such as my prep-school headmaster could have read to us as good clean fun the repellent (and terribly violent) works of Sapper and Dornford Yates.

Where Johns is objectionable is when it comes to race and nationalism. For most of the time this is comic to the extent of self-parody but (as with the *Sun* newspaper) it is so pervasive, so mindless, so unfeeling and uncaring that sooner rather than later it becomes very offensive indeed. Johns claimed to have as many white villains as coloured, and it is true that in one story the murderer of a young policeman turns out to be the village parson, incriminated by fingerprints taken from his own pulpit. This is a very rare case of a Johns villain being British. Many of the villains may be white (this was the distinction Johns was making), but they are still foreigners. He was not so much racist as unthinkingly xenophobic in the way of Alf Garnett, Henry Root and the *Sun*.

"I didn't care much for the chap. He was a shifty-eyed oily-looking type." "I see. He wasn't British."(*Biggles Forms a Syndicate,* 1961). Of a crook: "He did not look truly European." Those who are not British are dagoes, half-castes and wogs. Coolies are "yellow-faced tadpoles" and when abroad "the jabber of foreign languages fell on his ears; the reek of garlic hung in the dust-laden air." Huns are oily-faced and have close-cropped hair. Greeks are excitable, the Spanish are lazy and Italians are spaghetti-wallahs. (In recent editions niggers have been changed to savages, and references to Jews, half-breeds and half-castes have been circumvented. The editor of the recent Red Fox series of reprints says that about 20 changes a book were needed.)

Not only do individuals conform to their national stereotypes but go to extreme lengths to do so. When Lal Din plunges a knife into himself and drags it across his stomach Biggles remarks, "That should settle any doubts about his nationality. Only a Japanese would commit hara-kiri." Wouldn't it have been less drastic for Lal Din just to show his passport like anyone else?

Even inanimate objects have national characteristics: "A taxi whirled round the corner in a typically French fashion." As for garlic, this is something Johns mentions more often than is quite rational in anyone other than a cookery writer.

In the first few pages of *Biggles and Co* we meet a firm called Cronfeld & Carstairs. This gives away the whole plot. Even if you've never heard of Beachcomber's Big White Carstairs you know that anyone with that name is as surely a good egg as if his name was Carruthers. Whereas someone with a name like Cronfeld might as well go around with a notice saying "I am a foreigner and a crook." And so it proves.

But Johns is full of surprises. In *Biggles in the South Seas* he writes "A hundred years ago there were more than a thousand people on this island; now there aren't more than two hundred. The rest have died from the diseases white men have brought." And in the very last Biggles book *(Biggles Does Some Homework)* his successor is appointed. He is a young black man.

"To the younger male generation," Johns wrote,

> these stories satisfy the healthy natural craving for the thrills which were once supplied by stories of redskins, pirates and man versus beast. They know that the redskin and the pirate have gone for ever, and the wild beast nearly so; but the aeroplane lives. So hero-worshipping youth turns his eyes upwards and visualises himself in the cockpit of the fighting plane that wings its way across the sky. The glorious romance of air fighting probably stands out far more clearly on the printed page than ever it did in actual practice.

After the Blitz and Hiroshima and Dresden and Vietnam and the Gulf War, what Johns called "the glorious romance of air fighting" is not so much tarnished as obscene. And so it is with other values the virtue of which Johns took for granted. Geoffrey Trease wrote in 1978 about the Biggles books:

> They often express chauvinistic sentiments and an aggressive conviction of British and white superiority which are unacceptable today. It may well be that in years to come they will be read chiefly by half-incredulous research students, investigating the social values prevalent in children's fiction during the second quarter of the 20th century.

Modern editions of Johns's books remove references to coons, niggers, half-castes and dagoes. This destroys their documentary value as historical evidence. Cosmetically Bowdlerised versions are hypocritical and falsify the record. If whisky can be turned into lemonade and niggers can be written out of the script, then one day the wheel of correctness may demand that Johns says that Franco was a good guy.

* * * *

William Earl Johns was born in February 1893, and claimed to have been in the Royal Flying Corps at Miranshah in 1924, dropping bombs on tribesmen on the Northwest Frontier. This is precisely what my father (just ten years younger than Johns) did. After I wrote about Biggles in 1992 I sent the article to my father. His reply casts some doubt yet again on Johns's reliability. It also gives an authentic flavour of those early days of war-planes.

"Very interesting about 'Captain' W.E. Johns," he writes. "I was at Miranshah in 1924 and no sign of Johns. I flew from Miranshah to Peshawar on 12 November 1924, and celebrated my 21st birthday. I must work it out when I arrived. Entered RAF 1923 April. To India September 1924 to Miranshah.

"Shortly before I arrived, there had been a balls-up and tragedy. The squadron had been bombing a tribe in the hills. Squadron-Leader Capel commanding. A Wing-Commander Walser came to command. One day there was cloud and Capel said that it was not safe to go. Walser said, "Are you afraid?" So Capel saluted and took his squadron off. The clouds came down whilst the squadron was in the valley. Some flew into the hills and killed themselves. Capel crash-landed in the valley he was bombing and was captured and held for ransom. The ransom was paid and he came back to command the squadron. Johns may have been there before I arrived, and had left."

In another letter, a few days later, my father writes:

"Miranshah is at the head of the Tochi valley and at an entrance to a pass leading into Afghanistan. About four weeks after I arrived at Miranshah a tribe that had been in revolt with the Amir of Afghanistan, came down past us into India, as it was then all called. We heard rifle fire, but they were not pursued beyond the frontier. My recollection after nearly 70 years is that they came with camels with hens tied on.

"The reason that we bombed tribes and valleys is as follows. There was a Backward policy, with our frontier to be at the Indus, and a Forward policy to control up to the Afghan frontier, which is mountainous. An attempt was made to do the Forward policy by paying the tribes to keep order themselves. Picket posts were provided and garrisoned. In this instance the picket post had been butchered and their arms (muskets) had been taken. A fine was imposed, and rifles were to be returned. In the old days non-compliance would have been dealt with by sending a contingent that would have been sniped at by anyone with a gun, and nothing to achieve when they got there. So there was a new idea that the RAF should bomb them instead.

"I spent a few months doing this and there was nothing to bomb other than forts built of mud. Naturally they left their homes for caves during the hours that we might come. There was no sign that we ever did any damage at all or hurt anyone, but it had a nuisance value to them. We claimed to win, and I got a medal. Waziristan 19 — . I forget; lost the medal.

"My memory of going to India in a troopship in September 1923 is that all the deck space was available for the few officers and their wives, and that all the troops were confined below decks with only a tiny space available to them. We stopped at Port Said and I went ashore. On the way back to the boat the man rowing us demanded extra payment, but one of us produced a revolver and he rowed us both to the boat without argument. I had bought a bottle of some very potent liquid in Port Said and apart from feeling dreadful through the Red Sea I have no memory.

"We arrived at Bombay and some of us engaged a taxi to take us to the brothel area. I do remember one where there were very nice young girls or women, where we did not stay, and going later to a bungalow where there were older women. They seemed more like mothers to me, then aged twenty. I remained a virgin.

"Next was the train to Miranshah. There was one other officer going with me, older than me. He was called George — that was his surname. I think it was five days in the train and very hot. When we arrived at the Squadron at Miranshah, George and I were interviewed by Capel. I must have impressed him because he gave me lots of responsibilities, such as intelligence.

"Mother sent me from England some Yorkshire parkin which arrived in perfect condition after 6 weeks on the way.

"Quinlan arrived with a wooden leg; the good one was lost in the '14-18 war. The Air Vice-Marshal visiting wished to see any new pilots flying that had joined the Squadron since his last visit. There was only me and Quinlan. Quinlan spun into the deck so I landed and ran to his plane and pulled on his leg to get him out and it came off. It was the wooden leg. He was dead. Memorable.

"We were moved around frequently and it's quite likely that I was sent to Miranshah to replace Johns. He probably had a short service commission as I had. I got a permanent commission by passing an exam. Only twelve passed and I was 12th. Incredible that I should pass an exam."

My father's memory has not been blunted in his nineties. Since he remembers George, Walser, Capel and Quinlan by name, and since the Squadron was small, he would certainly have remembered Johns had he been there. If he replaced Johns he would surely have known the name of his predecessor. This was a tightly-knit group, with a high death-rate (more often on motor-bikes than in planes). I rather doubt if Johns was in Miranshah.

What my father's account certainly confirms is the outlook of those very young aviators, their language ("spun into the deck") and the contrast between their complete lack of sexual experience and their familiarity with war and death. The only bedtime lullaby I remember my father singing was a pastiche of "The Stalwart Lancer" called "The Young Aviator":

> As the young aviator lay dying (dying)
> And as on his death-bed he lay
> To the friends who around him were sighing
> (sighing)
> These last parting words he did say:
>
> Wrap me up in my tarpaulin jacket
> And say a poor buffer lies low
> And six stalwart airmen shall carry me
> With steps solemn, mournful and slow.
>
> Take the crankshaft out of my kidneys
> The joy-stick out of my brain
> From the small of my back take the con-rod
> And assemble the engine again.
>
> And at the Court of Inquiry
> If they ask for the reason I died
> Say I forgot that twice times iota
> Is the minimum angle of glide.

Guardian, *2nd July, 1992.*

WILLIAM THE CONQUEROR

Which of the following characters occurs in the works of P.G.Wodehouse? James B.("Rot-Gut") Ferret; Clarence Endive (who wore white knickerbockers, and had a fight with a man called Etty in the garden); Doctor Webster Civet; Jordan Baker (the lovely golf champion who was suspected of improving the lie of a ball during the semi-final of a tournament); the Blackbuck family, who "always gathered in a corner and flipped up their noses like goats at whosoever came near"; Mr Albrucksburger; Arditas Fitz-Peters; Brewer (who had his nose shot off in the war); G. Earl Muldoon (whose brother strangled his wife); Mr Schnellenhamer; Vera Prebble; Mr Zinnbaum?

Some are more obviously not P.G. Wodehouse than others. So, to put it another way, which of the above characters are (or are not) to be found in the works of F. Scott Fitzgerald? The lovely girl suspected of cheating at golf sounds like a suitable case for Jeeves to sort out and must surely be Wodehouse. Mustn't she? Just as G. Earl Muldoon whose brother strangled his wife sounds like Fitzgerald. But what about the knickerbockered Clarence Endive who fought a man called Etty in the garden? And the nose-flipping Blackbucks? In fact all of these characters are F. Scott Fitzgerald's and they all occur in *The Great Gatsby*, apart from Schnellenhamer, Prebble and Zinnbaum who are from Wodehouse's *Blandings Castle*.

I have only recently read H.G.Wells's remarkable novel *Tono-Bungay* (1909). Gatsby bears a striking similarity to Ponderevo, the self-made man who has risen to vast wealth by dubious means. The conclusion of Fitzgerald's novel, about "the green light, the orgastic future that year by year recedes before us", ends with the famous "So we beat on, boats against the current, borne back ceaselessly into the past." This seems to be a variation on the last sentence of *Tono-Bungay:* "We are all things that make and pass, striving upon a hidden mission, out to the open sea."

Researching the influence of P.G.Wodehouse and H.G. Wells on F.Scott Fitzgerald is a project I am saving up for when I retire, but for the time being, here goes. Wodehouse (born 1881) was fifteen years older than Fitzgerald (1896). By the time *Gatsby* was published in 1926 Wodehouse had been going a long while and Fitzgerald had had ample time in which to assimilate him. In fact they had known one another for some years. To his stepdaughter Leonora (Snorky), Wodehouse wrote on 14 November 1923,

> I have also met Scott Fitzgerald. In fact, I met him again this morning. He was off to New York with Truex, who is doing his play, The Vegetable. I believe those stories you hear about his drinking are exaggerated. He seems quite normal, and is a very nice chap indeed. You would like him. The only thing is, he goes into New York with a scrubby chin, looking perfectly foul. I suppose he gets a shave when he arrives there, but it doesn't show him at his best in Great Neck. I would like to see more of him.

Fitzgerald's Jazz Age world of the idle rich — drinking too much, having clandestine love affairs, getting into scrapes — is a trans-Atlantic version of the world of Galahad, Bertie Wooster, Gussy Fink-Nottle and other Drones, and without the wit and wisdom of Mr Mulliner. Much of Fitzgerald is now almost unreadable (though not *Gatsby*), while Wodehouse still seems new-minted. (Even so, tiresome as Fitzgerald now seems, he has worn better than the braggart and superbore Hemingway.)

The influence of P.G.Wodehouse on Richmal Compton is harder to determine, but the author of the William books stands up to the comparison much better than Fitzgerald does. Crompton claimed to find Wodehouse unreadable but this isn't evidence that she didn't read him. Her memory on such matters was selective. She also claimed not to have read the works of Booth Tarkington, the American writer who was not only the author of *The Magnificent Ambersons* (which Orson Welles made into a film) but also three volumes of Penrod stories (no, not Pernod but Penrod).

The first of the Penrod books was published by Hodder and Stoughton in 1914, five years before William Brown's debut. Kay Williams (in the Crompton biography *Just — Richmal*) details some of the similarities between Penrod and William. Penrod Schofield is aged 11, as is William. Like William he has a 19-year-old sister, and he meets his friends in a stable. He drinks "lickrish water", and he has a dog called Duke, "undescriptive of his person, which was obviously the result of a singular series of misalliances". Evidently Duke has the same lack of pedigree and comes from the same kennel as William's Jumble.

"Invalids murmured pitifully as Penrod came within hearing; and people trying to think cursed the days that they were born when he went shrilling by...". "Inhabitants of the street along which William was passing hastily shut their front windows...". "Mr Schofield's version of things was that Penrod was insane. 'He's a stark, raving lunatic!' declared the father." "Inside the house, [William's] father... discoursed to his wife on the subject of his son... 'He's insane,' he said, 'stark, raving insane...'"

There are plenty of parallels between the Penrod and William stories to show that (whatever Crompton said) she had indeed read Tarkington. More important, perhaps, is the debt that both owe to Tom Sawyer and Huck Finn. And, as with Tarkington, it is hard to believe that Richmal Crompton was not influenced by Wodehouse. They have so much in common, from the impeccable craftsmanship of the plot-lines to their thumbnail mugshots. As another round of the game with which we started, Which of these is whose? Maisie Fellowes is "a roly poly of a girl, who bore a striking resemblance to Queen Victoria in her old age." "The boy's face closely resembled a ripe tomato with a nose stuck on it." The first is Crompton, the second Wodehouse.

Their worlds also resemble one another in basking in the same Utopian glow. "The setting sun had turned the sky to gold. There was a soft haze over all the countryside. The clear bird songs filled all the air, and the hedgerows were bursting into summer." *(Just-William)*. "Blandings Castle slept in the sunshine. Dancing little ripples of heat-mist played across its smooth lawns... The morning sunshine descended like an amber shower-bath on Blandings Castle".

This is the perpetual perfect weather of England's temperate climate, of Shakespeare's *Midsummer Night's Dream*, and the Forest of Arden, and of Belmont at the end of *The Merchant of Venice* (Belmont is clearly in England rather than Italy) and of Ben Jonson's "Penshurst" and of Arnold's *Scholar Gypsy* and *Alice in Wonderland* and *The Wind in the Willows* and *Three Men in a Boat* and *The House at Pooh Corner*. The weather in William's village may not be quite so consistently sunny as at Blandings Castle, but you can be sure that the Mistral has never blown in either of these enchanted places, and that the Earl of Emsworth will never do a van Gogh and cut off an ear to give to Aunt Agatha any more than William will make a similar gift to Violet Elizabeth Bott. Lord Emsworth and his prize pig the Empress of Blandings, William and his mongrel Jumble, these and all the other characters are inhabitants of the mythical Land of Cockayne. Their summers are those of a happy, and rural, childhood.

Whatever went into the making of Richmal Compton as a writer, her own influence has been enormous. Those who have paid tribute to her range from John Lennon to Alan Coren, Dennis Potter, Keith Waterhouse and Roald Dahl. It seems appropriate that among politicians it should be Denis Healey and Norman Tebbit who have expressed admiration. Beryl Cooke is another fan, and Miles Kington has said that the William books are simply the funniest ever written.

When I worked for the *Times Literary Supplement* in the Sixties the first piece I commissioned (for complicated reasons it actually appeared in *The Times*) was by my old Cambridge friend Simon Gray, at that time a post-graduate researching a never-to-be-completed thesis on Henry James. It was in a series of reassessments. Simon picked on Kingsley Amis's *Lucky Jim* and pointed out the direct line of descent from William Brown to Jim Dixon. You merely have to substitute cigarettes and beer for sweets and liquorice and Just William has become Lucky Jim. They are both bored by high culture and by class-rooms and lecture halls and concerts, they both dislike authority and both have problems with girls. The celebrated incident in which Dixon sets fire to the bedclothes and makes comically absurd attempts to conceal his misdeeds is pure William. When William reads his school report in advance of giving it to his parents, his blackest fears are justified.

> He had had wild notions of altering it. The word "poor" could, he thought, easily be changed to "good", but few of the remarks stopped at "poor", and such additions as "Seems to take no interest at all in this subject" and "Work consistently ill prepared" would read rather oddly after the comment "good".

The author of *Lucky Jim* would have spun this out for pages, and it would have been less funny. Amis does not benefit from a comparison with Richmal Compton. She is more economical, her plots are more ingenious and she can more often double you up with laughter. Amis moved steadily to the right as he became older and crustier, turning into a parody of himself. Richmal Crompton called herself a Conservative but didn't show much interest in politics.

William's political guide to the politics of the first half of the century is clear-cut:

> "There's Conservatives an' they want to make things better by keepin' 'em jus' like what they are now. An' there's Liberals an' they want to make things better by alterin' them jus' a bit, but not so's anyone'd notice, and there's Socialists an' they want to make things better by taking everyone's money off 'em, and there's Communists an' they want to make things better by killin' everyone but themselves."
>
> "I'm goin' to be one of them," said Ginger promptly.

An unfortunate aberration is the story "William and the Nasties". The word play (Nazi-nasty) doesn't come off at all and the story develops an anti-semitic angle. This story has been dropped from subsequent reprints, though apparently the Israeli publishers have kept it in the Hebrew edition. Wodehouse did much better with Sir Roderick Spode and his Black-shorts.

William temperamentally is as opposed to fascism as he is to Bolshevism or any other totalitarianism. Indeed he is an enemy of the State, for William and his friends are the Outlaws. William is both anarchic and an anarchist. He is the agent of chaos, a Lord of Misrule, the Trickster-figure of many world myths, a Till Eulenspiegel. Like Chaplin, like Jean Renoir's Boudu, like Tati's Monsieur Hulot, like Laurel and Hardy, William can enter scenes of propriety and order and effortlessly transform them into total confusion. William always comes out on top of the heap, while figures of authority are left looking foolish. William is truly subversive.

Michael Palin says (in his foreword to Kay Williams's *Just-Richmal*) that

> William's world was a world behind adults' backs, on the other side of garden walls; a world of misplaced ingenuity, of great schemes doomed to glorious failure, of enormous ambitions thwarted. Not necessarily irrelevant and childish for all this; in fact, I find the William stories convey much of what adult life is really all about. The course of the affairs of great men and institutions in the world today is all mapped out in the William books. (It is) also a hugely liberating world; a world of grubby noncomformity, of grazed knees, bad spelling and dams made out of sticks... his restless anarchic spirit should still be an inspiration to us all.

William defies authority at school, in the home and everywhere else. He draws up the battlelines in the very first story, "Rice-mould", where his attitude is that "no weapon of offence against the world in general, and his own family in particular, was to be despised." Here is an occasion on which his chosen weapon is mimicry. For this purpose he listens to and commits to memory the conversation between his older sister Ethel and her friends.

> "Oh, *how* are you, Mrs Green?... And how's the darling baby? Such a duck! I'm dying to see him again! Oh Delia, darling! There you are! So glad you could come! What a perfect darling of a dress, my dear! I know whose heart you'll break in that! Oh, Mr Thompson!" — here William languished, bridled and ogled in a fashion seen nowhere on earth except in his imitations of his sister when engaged in conversation with one of the male sex. If reproduced at the right moment, it was guaranteed to drive her to frenzy.

When William first appeared in that story in 1919 he was aged eleven, an age at which he remained for the next 50 years. Likewise his sister Ethel remained stuck at nineteen. It is not clear whether Robert and Ethel were twins because sometimes Robert is also nineteen but at other times he is as young as seventeen or as old as twenty-one.

Whatever the case William was eleven and sufficiently younger than his toffee-nosed siblings to have been obviously an afterthought in Mr and Mrs Brown's family planning. On reflection he was probably not an afterthought: it would be more in character for William simply to be a mistake.

If William was eleven in 1919, then he was born in 1908, as were Simone de Beauvoir, Bette Davis, James Stewart, Ian Fleming, Osbert Lancaster and Lyndon Johnson. That year was also notable for a 70-minute flight by Orville Wright, the birth of Cubism, the appearance of the Model-T Ford, the publication of *The Wind in the Willows,* Northcliffe's acquisition of *The Times*, Belgium's annexation of the Congo and Austria's of Bosnia and Herzogovina. Also in 1908 the wife of Enrico Caruso ran off with another man, causing the great tenor to remark that it was just what he had been hoping for.

William has very much the leading role in the stories, but there is a huge cast of supporting (or opposing) characters. There are the other Outlaws, and enemies like the odious Hubert Lane (surely a prototype for Anthony Powell's Widmerpool and the former Home Secretary Mr Michael Howard). William's father, Mr Brown, is constantly enraged with his younger son, but quite often lets slip evidence that he might have once been a bit of a William himself. The long-suffering Mrs Brown is forever mending socks. Every eligible young man in the village instantly succumbs to the charms of William's sister Ethel, while his brother Robert immediately, shyly and ineptly falls for every girl in sight. Between them Ethel and Robert's male and female contemporaries add a large number of minor characters to the books. Then there are aunts and schoolteachers and neighbours and artists and poets and cops and robbers and (in the war) ARP wardens.

Crompton's portraits of minor characters can be deadly. None more so than Anthony Martin (a parody of A. A. Milne's Christopher Robin): there's an element of real, healthy hatred in the refrains "Anthony Martin is milking a cow," surpassed only by "Anthony Martin is doing his sums." Crompton's ear for conversation is faultless, as in William's mimicry above, and there are many writers considered greater who have never produced a sentence to match Richmal Crompton's "Mrs Beverton had embarked on a sea of prattle.".

Richmal Crompton wrote that William "dislikes little girls, not only because he considers them to belong to an inferior order of being but also because he suspects them of being allies of the civilization that threatens his liberty." This is true — in theory. In practice William is just as susceptible as his brother Robert. When William meets the schoolteacher Miss Drew, "William the devil-may-care pirate and robber-chief, the stern despiser of all things effeminate, felt the first dart of the malicious blind god. He blushed and simpered." Nor shall ever be forgotten Violet Elizabeth Bott and her golden curls.

> Violet Elizabeth Bott was a maiden of six years, with a lisp, an angelic face and a will of iron. She cultivated and used for her own purpose a scream that would have put a factory siren to shame and which was guaranteed to reduce anyone within ten yards of it to quite an expensive nervous breakdown.

Violet Elizabeth makes quick work of William. "Don't you like little girlth?" she said. "Me?" said William with superior dignity. "Me? I don't know anything about 'em. Don't want to." All she has to do is shed a tear or threaten to scream and scream till she's sick and he gives in. "'Kith me'", she said raising her glowing face. William was broken. He brushed her cheek with his."

How are the mighty fallen. In "William and the Parsons' Guy" Serena

> had dark hair, blue eyes and a wistful mouth. William had always prided himself on being a woman-hater, but despite his recent disillusionment at Anthea's hands he still found it hard to resist little girls with dark hair, blue eyes and wistful mouths. In order to conceal his weakness he glared at her ferociously.

Joan next door worships William. Amazingly the feeling is mutual. "'I like you better than any insect, Joan', he said generously. 'Oh, William, do you really?' said Joan, deeply touched." With Bettine Franklin he goes even further. He *gives her a centipede*.

William's schoolmasters are often absent. This is understandable since naturally they suffer frequent nervous breakdowns. In addition during the war many of them are called up for military service.

> The younger masters at William's school had vanished gradually with the course of the war, to be replaced by older men emerging often from the retirement of years. The new Maths master was half blind, and the new French master was more than half deaf, and the new Latin master so stiff with rheumatism that he could only walk with a stick. All three were such easy game that it was hardly worth trying to rag them.

That is how I remember schoolteachers of the immediate post-war period. If the picture of this decrepit crew seems cruel, one must remember that Richmal Crompton was herself a schoolteacher who walked with a stick, her leg having been paralysed by polio in early adulthood.

Photographs of her show a humorous but very determined person. In one of her numerous adult novels (*Matty and the Dearingroydes*, 1956) occurs the following. "Don't be ridiculous," said Honoria impatiently. "One must *learn* to snub people who waste one's time, if one's to make anything of life. Spineless amiability gets one nowhere." That could come from one of Jane Austen's letters.

Richmal Crompton was born in 1890 and died in 1969. Though certainly not spinelessly amiable she was, says her biographer Mary Cadogan, "immensely likeable — so likeable, indeed, that she is something of a biographer's nightmare. Despite attempts to provide a rounded-out and complete picture, it has been impossible to find anyone who has negative words to say about her!" She won a scholarship at Royal Holloway College, London University, and read classics, which she taught until her writing gave her financial independence. In addition to more than 30 William books she wrote more than 40 adult novels. I've only tried reading two of them: they weren't terribly good or terribly bad.

The illustrator of the William stories was Thomas Henry Fisher, who signed himself Thomas Henry. He was born in Eastwood, Nottinghamshire, in the house opposite the one in which D.H. Lawrence was born six years later. By then the Fisher family had moved, and there is nothing to suggest that the two ever met. It's a great pity: the idea of Thomas Henry illustrating *Women in Love* or *Lady Chatterley's Lover* is enchanting.

When Henry started illustrating William he was nearly 40. He and Richmal Crompton didn't meet in person till 1954 by which time he had been illustrating William for 35 years. He died suddenly at the age of 83 having just finished a William drawing. His 43 years' collaboration with Richmal Crompton lasted longer even than the Biggles one of W.E. Johns and Stead (24 years) though not as long as the Bunter one of Frank Richards and Chapman (more than 50 years). As with Lewis Carroll and Tenniel, or Ronald Searle and Geoffrey Willans, it is hard to think of the writing of Richmal Crompton without the drawings of Thomas Henry.

When I recently returned to the world of William it was after absenting myself for decades — since the days when the headmaster of my prep school would read them to us with tears of laughter running down his cheeks. I did so with some hesitation, reluctance even. I didn't want to spoil those happy childhood memories. Would the books stand up to re-reading? It took only a few pages to find that indeed the world of William is not as funny as I had remembered. It is far, far funnier, and far more disruptive.

Guardian, *8th October, 1992.*

IN THE GARDEN OF GIORGIO BASSANI

Giorgio Bassani's name will always be linked with those of two others, one an old Sicilian aristocrat called Giuseppe Tomasi, Duke of Palma and Prince of Lampedusa, the other a young Jewish girl called Micòl.

Bassani's only meeting with Lampedusa was at the San Pellegrino Literary Festival in 1954. The great poet Eugenio Montale had been invited to introduce to the public a promising, up-and-coming poet of his choice. Montale had recently received some poems by a Sicilian called Lucio Piccolo. Montale was impressed and, knowing nothing about him, invited Piccolo to the Festival.

There was widespread speculation about the identity of Montale's discovery. By the time the rumour-mill had done its work everyone was expecting a young man of dazzling Mediterranean good looks and wearing (according to *Paris-Match*) blue jeans. The real Piccolo, the one who got off the train from Sicily, was different. He was in his fifties, about Montale's age in fact. In true Sicilian style he was wearing a dark suit, and he was a Baron. Bassani recalls Piccolo's shyness and modesty, his surprise at the fuss that was being made of him, and at the same time his aristocratic air of *gran signore.*

Piccolo had not come alone. He brought with him a cousin even older than himself (a Prince, no less), and they had a man-servant with them too. The pallor of the rather flabby Sicilian aristocrats contrasted with the deeply sunburnt features of the servant, who was built like a blacksmith and never for a single moment let the old gentlemen out of his sight.

Bassani says the bizarre Sicilian trio were the hit of the Festival. He remembers Piccolo's cousin as having been tall, portly, silent and distinguished-looking, rather like a retired General. Although it was mid-summer he wore a hat and overcoat, and walked with a stick. When he was introduced to someone, he would just incline his head and say nothing. And that was Bassani's one and only encounter with Lampedusa in the flesh.

The San Pelegrino Festival kicked the Prince into action. He had not been impressed by the writers he met there and was sure he could write as well as any of them. And if cousin Lucio could win a prize then it was a "mathematical certainty" that he could too. For 25 years he had been talking about writing a historical novel set in Sicily in Garibaldi's time. Now he would do so.

The chapters poured out, with an increasing sense of urgency as Lampedusa became aware that he did not have long to live. Less than two years after San Pellegrino he sent the manuscript of *The Leopard* to the publishers Mondadori, where it was read by Elio Vittorini. Vittorini was also a Sicilian and a novelist but that was about all he did have in common with Lampedusa. Vittorini's father was a railwayman and his working life had started on a building site. He was a politically committed left-winger and his explicitly neo-realist and experimentalist programme for Italian literature had no room in it for an old-fashioned historical novel about the aristocracy. Predictably he turned *The Leopard* down.

The book was sent to another publisher, Einaudi. It so happened that Vittorini combined being a reader for Mondadori with being a director of Einaudi, so he was able to turn the book down again. The letter of rejection arrived on July 18, 1957, and four days later, at the age of 60, Lampedusa died.

Bassani has always been an admirer of Benedetto Croce. "My religion is that of liberty," he said when I talked to him in Rome. "I believe in liberty like a religion. In this respect I am a follower of Croce." And it was Croce's daughter Elena, who was a literary agent, who in 1958 gave Bassani a typescript. She wondered if it might be suitable for the series of books by modern writers that Bassani was editing for Feltrinelli. She had been sent it by a friend in Sicily about a year ago, since when it had just been lying about. She didn't know who it was by. Bassani started reading. Long before he realised that the author was Piccolo's silent cousin at San Pellegrino he knew he was reading one of the masterpieces of modern Italian — indeed, European — literature.

Bassani immediately visited Lampedusa's widow in Palermo, where he found further manuscripts. While expressing admiration for the book he told the Princess that he felt something was missing at the end. She thought Lampedusa had written a chapter about a ball shortly before he died. Bassani finally tracked down the whereabouts of what is perhaps the most celebrated chapter in the novel. Then Lampedusa's adopted son came up with another chapter. And so on.

Preparing a single text out of a number of manuscripts and typescripts involved Bassani in making countless decisions which will keep textual scholars busy forever. What is beyond question is that he edited the book brilliantly. It is a rare piece of good fortune that Lampedusa's disordered and scattered pages should have passed through the hands of someone who was himself a great poetic novelist.

Only nine months after Bassani received the anonymous manuscript, *The Leopard* was published. It was disliked in many quarters. Sicilians thought it showed Sicily in a poor light, Roman Catholics thought it showed Roman Catholics in a bad light. The avant-garde complained that it was old-fashioned, while the Left noted with equal perception that it was not a neo-realist account of the class struggle as experienced by the oppressed industrial proletariat of Turin (or words to that effect).

In fact *The Leopard* didn't really have anything to offer anyone — except, that is, those who (as Montale shrewdly pointed out) had sworn never again to open an Italian novel. And they were out there in droves. Within a year *The Leopard* was reprinted 57 times, and was soon translated into more than 20 languages and was a major international film production (directed by Visconti, starring Burt Lancaster, Alain Delon and Claudia Cardinale). It was hailed in Italy by Montale, in England by E.M. Forster and in France (to the chagrin of the comrades) by the impeccably left-wing Louis Aragon. The claustrophobic Italian literary world didn't know what had hit it.

As though Bassani's part in the success of *The Leopard* was not enough, he followed it up, this time with a novel of his own. As with *The Leopard*, the Italian Left and avant-garde took a dim view of *The Garden of the Finzi-Continis* and for much the same reasons. Again it was Montale who hit the nail on the head. He said the great thing about the characters in *The Garden of the Finzi-Continis* is that none of them has read Robbe-Grillet.

In fairness it should be said that Leonardo Sciascia (who attacked *The Leopard* when it came out) later publicly retracted, just as Umberto Eco (who was originally against *The Garden of the Finzi-Continis*) later changed his mind. The general reading public had no need for such U-turns. It was entranced from the start, and continues to be. Hard-boiled eggs who have resisted the charm of *Brideshead* without even trying, have had only to step into the Finzi-Contini world to be spellbound. Their garden is every bit as dangerous as Mr McGregor's was to Peter Rabbit. And most bewitching of all is the beautiful, unobtainable, doomed Micòl, to whom the book is dedicated.

Bassani draws you into his world and makes you read as a participant. The effect is distressing. As the narrator's calm voice tells us about these young people (expelled from the Ferrara tennis club because they are Jews, and invited to use the private court of the hugely rich Finzi-Continis), about their bicycle rides and telephone conversations, their studies and exam results, their hopes and fears, their loves, their successes and disappointments, we want to cry out loud because *we know what is going to happen*. And we know what is going to happen because Bassani tells us right at the beginning. The Fascists are going to deport them to Germany and they are going to die in the gas chambers.

From that account Bassani's book may sound like Isherwood's *Goodbye to Berlin* (and the film *Cabaret* based on it). Bassani is much more intelligent and more complex than Isherwood, but there are similarities in these stories of young love set against a background of growing Fascism. This, and the seductive glow of nostalgia, are brilliantly caught in Vittorio de Sica's film of *The Garden of the Finzi-Continis*.

Bassani has made no secret of his dislike of the film and it is easy to see why. The end of the book is ambiguous both about Micòl's conduct and her character: the end of the film makes explicit what the book leaves in doubt. As for the novel's all-important introductory chapter, de Sica simply leaves it out. It is a beautiful film but the beauty is all that de Sica does catch. The book is far richer than that, working simultaneously on several levels with the complexity of great poetry, and imagery of Shakespearean resonance. It is a love story, it is an account of the impact of Fascism on Italian Jewry, and it is also a complex investigation of the universal themes of past, present and future, of life and death.

The Finzi-Continis are every bit as decadent and *fin de race* as Lampedusa's House of Salina. Tancredi tells the Prince that "If we want things to stay as they are, things will have to change." The Finzi-Continis do not want to change. "They are dead," Bassani says firmly. "Obsessed with their house, their garden, art, the past and memories, if they are not dead what are they?" Shockingly he suggests (indeed virtually states) that the Italian Jews were accomplices in their own downfall. He says that with himself as virtually the only exception, all the Jews in Ferrara were Fascists until they were expelled from the party. Not that this was to save them. Half of Ferrara's Jewish community was deported to Germany. Only three came back.

Bassani insists that *The Garden of the Finzi-Continis* should not be seen in isolation. It is part of a larger work.

He has revised and collected together all the Ferrara books in one massive volume, and says that *Il Romanza di Ferrara* should be read from beginning to end in the correct order.

This seems to me a council of perfection. Ideally we should doubtless read Dante straight from beginning to end, but few of us are going to do so. But Bassani has a point. Since his novels all bear what might be called a family likeness, the variations become very important. They are all concerned with Fascism and the Jewish community in Ferrara in the 1930s and during and immediately after the War. The furniture of the novels doesn't vary much from one to another: there's almost always a cemetery or a tombstone or a memorial, there are young people with bicycles and tennis and telephones and books, there's the train between Bologna and Ferrara. These and a few other simple motifs prove as endlessly permutable as the simple vases and bottles in the still life paintings of Giorgio Morandi. (Like Morandi, Bassani is a native of Bologna and his admiration for the painter is such that he has actually called himself a disciple).

It is perhaps relevant to the work of both of them that what in English is called "still life" in Italian is *morta natura*, dead nature. What Bassani said of the Finzi-Continis, that they are dead, goes for his other characters. They are on the margin of society. Some (like Lida Mantovani) barely exist; some are killed right at the beginning, the rest being flash-back; one of them simply disappears; some are suicides; one of them is catatonic; one actually comes back from the dead (returning from Germany in 1943 and assumed to have perished in the gas chambers, he finds his name embarrassingly included in a plaque commemorating the victims). They are all lost souls.

The exception is the narrator, the *io*, the "I". Almost the first thing Bassani said to me was that this person is the most important character in his work. Who is this "I"? Is he Bassani, or is he a modern Dante in an Inferno that is Ferrara? Is Micòl his Beatrice? Who is Micòl?

Bassani's Ferrara, whether or not it is Inferno as well, is certainly Ferrara. I don't think I would have recognised Ferrara from the paintings that de Chirico was producing there around the time Bassani was born, but Bassani's descriptions are accurate down to the last arcade, street sign, bicycle and cemetery. (In the Jewish cemetery I found within minutes a number of Finzi graves, quite close to a number of Continis, but no Finzi-Continis; fiction has to start somewhere).

In the film the central character is called Giorgio, which is just another little subtlety that de Sica crunches. In the books the "I" is never named, which is even more self-effacing than Proust, who refers to Marcel twice. Nevertheless the novels contain so much autobiographical material that clearly Giorgio Bassani overlaps a great deal with the narrator.

Giorgio Bassani was born in 1916 to a prominent Jewish family of Ferrara. His father was qualified in medicine but had sufficient means not to need to practice. His home was in Ferrara, though he was actually born in Bologna and most of his further education was in Bologna, less than an hour away by train. In his imaginative landscape Ferrara, his home, stands for the heart; Bologna, the university, for the head. A frequent motif in his work is the train journey from one to the other.

Like other Jews, he and his family were persecuted under the racial laws. His first book appeared in 1940 under the pseudonym Giacomo Marchi. (The name of a Jew couldn't be printed even in a telephone directory, or in newspaper birth, marriage and death announcements).

In 1942 he became actively involved in anti-Fascist activities, and was arrested, imprisoned and released with the fall of Fascism. He married, left Ferrara, was active in the Resistance. After the war he lived in Rome with his wife and two children, worked as a translator (Hemingway's *Farewell To Arms*), wrote film scripts and taught. From 1948 to 1969 he edited the distinguished international literary journal *Botteghe Oscure*. He wrote journalism, published his poems, and the novels starting appearing in 1953. In the subsequent years, as well as writing novels and essays, teaching, and working for Feltrinelli, he was also for a while Vice-President of RAI (the equivalent of the BBC). He is also a founder, and is now President, of Italia Nostra, an organisation concerned with protecting Italy's countryside and its artistic and cultural heritage. Italia Nostra's offices are near Bassani's house in Rome and it was there that I met him.

He is still extremely good-looking, with the astonishingly blue eyes that in the novels earn the nickname "Celestino", heavenly blue. He holds himself very erect, but walks with difficulty. His manner switched disconcertingly between being tremendously courteous, polite, helpful and even friendly, and then at the next moment being — well, prickly. Fortunately our meeting began and ended in the friendly mode.*

One of the awkward moments came after he had said that the first person, "I", is the most important person in the book. I asked in my clumsy Italian if the "I" of the books is the same as the Dottore Bassani sitting here? The effect was extraordinary. "Dottore Bassani no," he said very sharply. "Professore Bassani. Dottore is ridiculous. A lot of people are Dottore. Professore is different."

So bang went that question. *Who's Who* in Italy has him as Dottore, but I didn't say so. Shortly afterwards he remembered that he had an appointment in ten minutes and we were heading for the door. Once outside he became utterly charming again, posing for photographs (for a while — then *"Basta"*, enough) signing the copies of his books I had brought with me and solicitously making sure I had found a taxi and then waving goodbye with a smile.

And Micòl? I turned up a 30-year-old article in *Corriere d'informazione* that quotes Bassani's mother saying

---

*I now (1997) realise that, sadly, I was witnessing the beginning of his mental deterioration. Bassani has been declared by a court to be legally incapable of running his own affairs.

"Micòl comes from the poetic imagination of my Giorgio. She is the concentrated ideal of the young women he knew and loved as he was growing up. Perhaps one of them had special importance. In fact Giorgio was engaged to a Catholic girl but it had to be broken off when the pitiless racial laws prohibited marriage between Jews and Christians." In the novels this is not what happens to the narrator but to his alter ego, Bruno Lattes. While Bassani insisted to me that everything in his books is true he also said that he had invented Micòl. He said he identified himself with Micòl. "Micòl is like me."

Flaubert said *"Madame Bovary, c'est moi."* Perhaps we should leave it at that. These questions are fascinating but in the end a distraction. All that really needs saying on the occasion of his 75th birthday is that Giorgio Bassani is one of the great witnesses of this century, and one of its great artists.

Guardian, *March 7th, 1991*

THE BEST AIR IN THE WORLD

Some of the paper on my desk has gone undisturbed for decades. During recent tentative preliminary excavations I came across a cutting from the *Guardian* dated 25 May 1972. It concerned the village of Norton Bavant in Wiltshire which had just held its first Parish Council meeting for 80 years. Jesse Brake, aged 65, retired farmer, had been elected Secretary. Then, *since nobody had anything to say*, they had adjourned for a year. Mr Brake commented, "I suppose it indicates that nothing special or exciting has happened in the village over the last 80 years."

Quarter of a century has passed since then. What has happened in Norton Bavant in that time? Does the Parish Council now meet regularly and often? Do they vote on party political lines? Are there fiercely contested elections with door-to-door canvassing, dirty-tricks departments, spin-doctors and image consultants? Do they raise taxes and make rules and issue orders telling people what they can and can't do? Or has nothing special or exciting continued to happen in the village? Is it an anarchist utopia, living happily without government? Whatever the answers, Norton Bavant must surely hold lessons for all of us.

Finding the village on the Ordnance Survey map is easy enough. It's on the very edge of Salisbury Plain, in the Wylye Valley near Warminster. Finding it on the ground is not so easy. A sign at the side of the road says NORTON BAVANT, then there's a bus-stop, and then on the other side of the road is the back of the sign announcing NORTON BAVANT to those approaching from the opposite direction. If you blinked then you missed the minor road turning off.

This leads to the hamlet, a few houses scattered round a meadow full of grazing cows. There's a manor house, and a church, and farm buildings, thatched houses, and some post-war in-filling. There used to be more thatched houses, as the oldest inhabitant, Miss Ewan, remembers well. It was the day France fell, she says, and Albert's wife caught the frying-pan on fire and of course it was thatch and these two cottages burnt down, and the firemen came with their hoses, one each side squirting water at one another over the top of the roofs.

In Miss Ewan's parlour there's a grandfather clock ticking and a kettle always near the boil next to the open fire. She has a twinkle in her eye, and just a trace of her original northern accent. When she left home she planned to work her way round the world, staying a year or two in each place. Norton Bavant was her first stop, as housekeeper for Mr Drake, and that's as far as her globe-trotting got. She's been here ever since. That's 56 years.

The character of the village, past and present, is conveyed by the house names. The Old Vicarage, The Lodge, The Brewhouse, The Mill House, The Bungalow, Pillbox Cottage, The School House, Linden Lea, Middleton Farm House, North Farm, The Bothy, The Old Smith Cottage, The Moorings, Norton Bavant Manor (residence of Lady Priscilla and Sir John Jardine-Paterson).

The Electoral Register lists 98 names in 50 households. As in many English villages the population is lower now than at any time since the Black Death. In 1377 there were 94 poll-tax payers in Norton Bavant; in 1676 there were 196 adults; this rose to around 260 throughout the 19th century, down to 128 in 1951, and now under 100.

When Mr Drake (wrongly called Brake by the *Guardian*) said that nothing special or exciting had happened in the village over the past 80 years he could probably have added a nought, or even two. There are barrows, and Bronze Age and Roman remains, but nothing specially exciting about them. Things livened up after the Norman Conquest though, and to such an extent that the narrative in volume 8 of the *Victoria County History* becomes as complex as an opera synopsis. In 1355 Roger Bavant died and his estranged wife Hawise alleged that the property was entailed upon her and her issue, but the seal on the deed backing her claim was forged and when John (her son and heir) left for Italy to become a Franciscan friar, she withdrew it (the claim). So the King gave Norton Bavant to the Dominican nuns of Dartford who held it unmolested until the Dissolution.

This tale provides an Umberto Eco historical background, and there's a present-day cast that seems readymade for a classic English murder. This is the world of Miss Marple, Inspector Morse, P.D. James or Ruth Rendell, where Laura Ashley, Lapsang Souchong tea, homicide and good manners go hand in hand.

Roger Bavant was obviously bumped off, but whodunnit? Constable, assemble the usual suspects in the library, or in Miss Ewan's parlour, or if that's not big enough in a convenient room in the Manor House. Ancient and modern jostle together. We have the widow Hawise, Friar John, the unmolested nuns, the squire, the parson, the doctor, the butler, Sir John and Lady Priscilla, the farmer, the schoolmaster, the oldest inhabitant, the opera singer (a recent arrival), the Parish Clerk Gordon Evans (who has been so helpful in my inquiries, suspiciously helpful, you might think) and of course the incumbent Parish Chairman Edward Moore, a bearded lawyer of somewhat piratical demeanour. But, you protest, many of these weren't even born at the time of the murder. Precisely. The perfect alibi.

After the nuns' time the village became the property of the Benett family and remained so until this century, John Montagu Fane-Benett-Stanford dying in 1947 having outlived his children. At the beginning of the nineteenth century this was a Rotten Borough. John Benett, the Member of Parliament known as "Wiltshire Benett", was a brute who believed in starving the poor, hated the labourers, was attacked by them in the riots of 1830, and took an enthusiastic part in sentencing them to transportation.

Cobbett couldn't stand him and — glory be! — Cobbett rode through Norton Bavant. He spent the night in the inn at Heytesbury, a few minutes' walk from Norton Bavant which then as now has no inn. He probably stayed at the Angel, as I did, and can recommend as warmly as Cobbett extolled it to his readers in 1826. That's 170 years ago, but Cobbett is so immediate that as I sat in the inn and read his words I felt I could have put my hand out and have it crushed in his great fist.

Cobbett found some men and boys staying there who had been employed in the cloth factories at Bradford-on-Avon. Being out of work they had come here to get nuts.

> These poor nutters were extremely ragged. I saved my supper, and I fasted instead of breakfasting. That was three shillings which I had saved, and I added five to them, with resolution to save them afterwards, in order to give these chaps a breakfast for once in their lives.

Recognising his generosity, the landlord and landlady of the inn reduced his bill considerably. Cobbett's account ends with him "leaving the nutters at their breakfast, and very much delighted with the landlord and his wife."

Cobbett was an awkward old curmudgeon but here he's at his most attractive, and his good mood goes on. From Salisbury to Warminster

> The country is the most pleasant that can be imagined. Here is water, here are meadows; plenty of fresh-water fish; hares and partridge in abundance.... hills of every height, size, and form; valleys, the same; lofty trees and rookeries in every mile; roads always solid and good; always pleasant for exercise; and the air must be of the best in the world.

The country is "singularly bright and beautiful", and "going along the turnpike road, which runs between the lower fields of the arable land, you see the large and beautiful flocks of sheep upon the sides of the down, while the horn-cattle are up to their eyes in grass in the meadows." He declares Norton Bavant to be "one of the prettiest spots that my eyes ever beheld."

By the end of the century the power of the local tyrant had declined. Steven Hobbs, the archivist at County Hall, Trowbridge, dug out for me minutes of Norton Bavant Parish meetings. The earliest is December 4, 1894, and records in beautiful copper-plate handwriting that Mr John Hiscock of South Farm was elected Chairman by acclamation and no further business arising the Meeting was declared closed.

That set the pattern for subsequent meetings for the next 30 years. Then on 25 April, 1927, officers were elected, and there was a vote of thanks to Mr G.E. Rugg for his services for the past 23 years, his appointment as Rate Collector having been terminated under the new Rating Act. No other business arising, the Meeting was declared closed. These minutes are not signed for the evident reason that there was not a next meeting for them to be read at.

Then, as we have seen, the meetings resumed in April 1972. There were seventeen parishioners present, and the minutes show the *Guardian* was wrong in reporting that nobody had anything to say. On the contrary the Meeting resolved that the Clerk ask the County Council Divisional Survey to look into the following matters and take the necessary action: Road sweeping not being carried out; road flooding; ditches needing cleaning; road verges encroaching on road; footpath through the village getting overgrown.

The same issues recur in minutes for subsequent years: mostly it's draining and the need for GO SLOW signs. On Nov 1 1972 Mr Chatting drew the attention of the meeting to the *untidyness* of the village bus stop and the area around it. Mr Drake explained that he had been responsible for building the shelter which now belonged to Sir John Jardine-Paterson. It was not clear who was responsible for cleaning it.

The uneventfulness of the minutes is almost hypnotic. Year by year nothing special or exciting goes on happening. In 1977 Mr Moore raised the question of the new light which had been erected in the village and asked if anyone knew its purpose. In 1978 Mr Clark reported a letter asking whether the Parish wished to participate in the Best Kept Village Competition. Dr Bartholomew said it would be pointless to do so if our prospects were nil. This view was supported and it was agreed that no action be taken.

October 1990. Litter Bin. There was no further information.

March 1994. Matters Arising. A question was raised with regard to the hole outside No 7 Norton Bavant which was referred to in the Minutes of the previous meeting. It was agreed that this should be taken up with the Highways Authority.

Local Government Reorganisation. The Meeting conveyed a general concern that they did not have sufficient knowledge of the topic for them to come to a decision within the timescale set.

Neighbourhood Watch. Mr Gabbott had nothing to report on this topic. He assumed that the literature was being properly distributed. Reference was made to the Neighbourhood Watch sign which is coming adrift from the tree to which it was fixed. Mr Palmer undertook to pursue the matter.

And so it is, and so it was, and so it shall be. Small is beautiful, and this is minimalism brought to government. It's not actually a Parish Council but a Parish Meeting. This means they don't have elections: any parishioner who bothers to turn up can vote. There are usually about 20 people present, which (being one-fifth of the electorate) is a most impressive piece of participatory democracy in action. Nobody is paid, nobody claims expenses. They have the power to raise a precept (a local tax) but have never done so. Instead they raise money by barbecues and jumble sales and whip-rounds and donations, and they rely on volunteer work. They talk about drains and ditches, read the minutes of the last meeting and set the date of the next one. Gordon Evans, the Parish Clerk, says it's a forum where people can raise problems, and where they can collectively say thank-you to someone. "The world wouldn't stop without us," he says, "but it would be a less happy place."

Guardian, *2nd May, 1995*.

MERE ANARCHY

Anarchists are fond of paradoxes. They are challenging, they turn things upside down, they give a jolt to received ideas. Probably the best-known anarchist paradox is Proudhon's "Property is theft". Another is "Anarchy is Order." I even spotted this anarchist marker, which some say lies behind one of the most widespread of all graffiti — an O with an A in it — in Budapest on October 24, 1996, the 40th anniversary of the Hungarian uprising. After decades of Nazism and Stalinism and its inheritors, the Hungarian anarchist is a rare bird. But this is one of the characteristics of anarchism. It is like the plants that against all odds emerge through the slightest cracks in the concrete of an urban desert. Colin Ward, using a slightly different image, says that "an anarchist society, which organises itself without authority, is always in existence, like a seed beneath the snow." It is not so much a matter of survival as of apparently spontaneous regeneration.

Just as Molière's Monsieur Jourdain was astounded to learn that he had been speaking prose all his life, so there are many who to a greater or lesser extent are anarchists without knowing it. No account of anarchism could leave out Godwin (Shelley's father-in-law), Tolstoy, Thoreau or Gandhi, yet for various reasons none of them called himself an anarchist. The term is so routinely used as one of abuse that today many comrades call themselves libertarians. This strikes me as a bit like people who call themselves humanists or agnostics when all along they're honest-to-God atheists. Still, saying you're a libertarian does save time since it spares you yet another conversation on the lines of "No, I do not throw bombs, nor do I defend people who throw bombs. In fact, I'm pretty much a pacifist." (Not that all libertarians are pacifists). On the other hand the bonus of getting into that conversation is that you can point out that it's not anarchists who throw bombs but governments. All the explosives thrown at Heads of State by all the anarchists in the whole of history would add up to a fraction of the explosive destruction hurled by governments at whole civilian populations in a single hour — or minute — day after day, year after year. Their bomb-throwing is called peace-keeping.

Pierre-Joseph Proudhon (1809-1865) was the first person to call himself an anarchist, but ideas and behaviour exist independently of the labels that are put on them. Historians of anarchism customarily kick off much earlier than Proudhon. With the ancient Greeks, for example, such as the Stoic Zeno: as against Plato's authoritarian State with its man-made laws, Zeno proposed the idea of a society based on natural law with no police and no armies, temples, lawcourts, schools, money or marriage, where instead of compulsion there would be equality and freedom. Or Epictetus, who said "Do not wish to be a general, or a senator, or a consul, but to be free."

And there were the Cynics. The best-known was Diogenes, who lived in a tub — and why not? Alexander the Great tried to test Diogenes's simple-life philosophy by offering him anything he wanted. Diogenes said all he wanted was for Alexander to get out of his light. Well done. Diogenes's greatest admirer was Rabelais, who imagined the anarchist Abbey of Thelema where there is no poverty, chastity or obedience; the only rule is "Do what you will."

Or with Taoism. Lao Tzu (born 604 BC) wrote that "the more laws and restrictions there are, the poorer the people become. The sharper men's weapons, the more trouble in the land. The more ingenious and clever men are, the more strange things happen. The more rules and regulations, the more thieves and robbers." He believed that goodness comes from within and cannot be imposed. This was contrary to the teaching of Confucius who wanted good government. Centuries later we find the same argument in the newly-formed United States. Jefferson, who wrote the Declaration of Independence, announced in ringing tones that all men are created equal and independent. He also owned a very large number of slaves whom he exploited and kept in miserable conditions. Whereas (Confucius-like) Jefferson said that "That government is best which governs least," Thoreau (like Lao Tzu) replied that the best government is the one which doesn't govern at all.

Closer to home, modern anarchists can trace an ancestry back through William Morris, Godwin, the Levellers and Diggers to the Peasants' Revolt of 1381. In that mediaeval protest against the Poll Tax the part of Mrs Thatcher was played by John of Gaunt, that of First Peasant by Jack Straw (yes, really) and the meddlesome priest (the Robert Runcie of the day?) was John Ball. This "hedgerow priest" demanded of anyone in earshot

When Adam delved and Eve span,
Who was then the gentleman?

Adam is not the correct answer.

John Ball was an early class-warrior, but his famous question also draws attention to the fact that the original couple in the Garden of Eden were not only the ancestors of us all, rich and poor alike, but also that Adam and Eve were the first anarchists. God gave them only one order and they promptly broke it. He told them not to eat of the tree of the knowledge of good and evil (there is no mention of an apple in the Bible). Adam and Eve knew just what to do with an order. The correct procedure is as follows. First, question the order. Theirs was very much to reason why, and they did. If God seriously didn't want us to eat from that tree, why didn't he plant it somewhere else? And why, out of all the trees, did he specifically draw our attention to this one? Just asking for trouble. Apart from which, being able to tell the difference between right and wrong sounds like a good idea.

So, having weighed the order in the balance and found it wanting, Adam and Eve moved to step two. If an order is sensible (like "Mind the step" or "Shake well before using" or "Do not expose to naked flame") then you obey it. If the order is not sensible then you disobey it. Which they did.

We are going through a period in which politicians, priests and the press are agonising about how to find a basis for morality in the vacuum left by the collapse of religion. Most anarchists are non-believers and have thought about this subject for a long time. They do not see morality as a matter of obeying a code, either religious or legal. It is a matter of something (Original Virtue, perhaps) that comes from within. Like Lao Tzu, Rabelais believed that free people, "well-educated and keeping good company, have by nature an instinct and incentive which always encourages them to virtuous acts, and holds them back from vice."

The pillars of our community might just learn something from the anarchists on this subject. Instead one hears them on radio discussions talking about Original Sin and bringing back corporal or capital punishment, or both. Without meaning to be funny Professor Roger Scruton was a hoot on the subject of Original Sin on the radio the other day. If only Peter Cook were with us.

Even on their own terms the Christian moralists have got it wrong. They confuse sin with Original Sin. Morality is the ability to distinguish between good and evil. Adam and Eve in the Garden of Eden were, like the animals, innocent because they were amoral. They acquired morality (the ability to distinguish between g. and e.) precisely by disobeying God. In the Judaeo-Christian story, Original Sin is the very source of morality.

The recent code of the National Forum for Values in Education and the Community* is confused about all this.

---

* What ever happened to the National Forum?

At one moment it says that we should value the law, should obey the law and encourage others to do so. In the same breath it says we should "be ready to challenge values or actions which may be harmful to individuals or communities". What if the law is harmful? The recent Ploughshares case concerned four women who took hammers and did massive damage to a Hawk fighter aircraft intended for the use of the Indonesian government in repressing the people of East Timor. The women made no attempt to conceal their actions. Their destruction of property was clearly illegal, but the jury evidently shared the women's view that the law of conscience is higher than the law of the land, and acquitted. This is in line with the principle of the Nuremberg judgments. The Holocaust was the work of authoritarian, disciplined, obedient people. Whatever you may think of anarchists, there is one excuse they will never make: they will never say "I was only obeying orders."

Paradise Lost begins with the words "Of man's first disobedience..." Milton was fiercely protestant in every sense, and anti-monarchist. In his great poem his sympathies — whatever his conscious intentions — are not imaginatively on the side of the angels (a dull lot). The hero is the glamorously dashing Satan. And Milton says something very curious in his introductory lines. His aim, he says, is "to justify the ways of God to Men." Why should Milton have felt that God's ways needed justifying?

Thoreau wrote a pamphlet "On the Duty of Civil Disobedience" and indeed went to jug (albeit for only one night) for refusing to pay his Poll Tax as a protest against the United States' imperialistic war in Mexico. (From the Peasants' Revolt to the present day Poll Taxes have been a fertile source of recruits to anarchism.) Walt Whitman admired Thoreau for his "lawlessness — his dissent — his going his absolute own road hell blaze all it chooses." Dissent, disobedience, bloody-mindedness, insubordination, call it what you like — it is something for the anarchist to admire. Galileo, Martin Luther, Martin Luther King —

they weren't all anarchists but they were disobedient. Gandhi was extremely disobedient, and he beat the British Empire (with a lot of help from his friends, trained in disobedience).

Oscar Wilde, who could hardly open his mouth without a paradox coming out, said that "Disobedience, in the eyes of anyone who has read history, is man's original virtue. It is through disobedience that progress has been made, through disobedience and rebellion." His *The Soul of Man Under Socialism* was translated into many languages and widely read in Tsarist Russia. Shaw mocked Wilde's political ideas. Shaw was a wise and witty man but he got it badly wrong when with the Fabian Webbs he whitewashed Stalin's Russia. This is not something Wilde or any other anarchist would have done, and Wilde's ideas seem to be standing the test of time better than those of the founders of the Labour Party, let alone the Bolsheviks. Now that Clause IV has gone there would be nothing left in today's Blairite new Labour even for Shaw, let alone William Morris.

In his indispensable history of anarchism, *Demanding the Impossible* (Fontana),* Peter Marshall calls Oscar Wilde the greatest of all libertarians. Wilde himself said in an interview in France in 1894 that "I am rather more than a Socialist. I am something of an Anarchist, I believe, but of course the dynamite policy is absurd."

The popular idea of an anarchist is still that of a man in a broad-brimmed hat with a smouldering bomb under his cloak. This image has been reinforced by countless cartoonists as well as such major writers as Conrad *(The Secret Agent)*, Dostoevsky *(The Possessed)* and, slightly improbably, Henry James *(The Princess Casamassima)*. It is not without historical basis. A century ago anarchists of the nihilist persuasion and exponents of what was called

---

* *Another highly recommended history of anarchism is the much shorter* Anarchy: a graphic guide, *succinctly written and boldly illustrated by Clifford Harper, Camden Press.*

Propaganda of the Deed did perpetrate acts of extreme violence, including the assassination of various heads of State. Many anarchists (the overwhelming majority, I believe) detest violence and (like Oscar Wilde) would distance themselves from the "dynamite policy". But this is not something that can simply be written out of anarchist history. Having conceded this, an anarchist would point out that these isolated acts of violence are minimal compared with the consistent violence of the State. There is no need to list the huge-scale horrors of this century. They have all been perpetrated by governments, not one by anarchists.

Anarchists come in all shapes and sizes. There are anarcho-communists, anarcho-syndicalists, pacifist anarchists, Christian anarchists, individualist anarchists, mutualists... the list could go on for ever because there are as many sorts of anarchist as there are anarchists. There is no membership, no text or manifesto that must be adhered to, no formal organisation.

So who are the anarchists? The nearest thing I know to sociological analysis is the readership surveys carried out by *Freedom*. This consistently lively, thought-provoking and provocative journal can hardly be found in newsagents. Subscriptions are £14 a year, from Freedom Press in Angel Alley, 84b Whitechapel High Street, London E1, and there's also an excellent theoretical quarterly called *The Raven* (£12 a year). Climb the rickety stairs of Angel Alley and you find the best shop for libertarian literature anywhere. I once bought a copy of George Woodcock's magazine *Now* published during the war with contributions by the likes of George Orwell, Herbert Read and Alex Comfort. More than twenty years later they were still selling it at its original cover price — sixpence, I think. One of the founders of *Freedom* 110 years ago was the great anarchist Prince Peter Kropotkin (who, incidentally, wrote the excellent entry on anarchism in the 1911 edition of *Encyclopedia Britannica*).

These surveys are far from comprehensive since *Freedom's* small circulation must be only a fraction of the anarchist population, self-styled or not. Still, it is at least something to go on. The survey in the 1960s showed that out of 457 who replied: 40 were engaged in industry, and six of these were managers; 23 worked on the land, of whom 8 owned their own farms and one was an estate manager; 19 worked in communications and transport. That made up 15 per cent of the sample who belonged to the traditional anarchist ranks of workers and peasants (hammer and sickle). On the other hand there were 52 teachers, 30 students, 20 architects, 16 journalists and writers, 23 in arts and entertainment, 12 in publishing, 25 in scientific research, 25 in health and welfare, 40 in administrative and clerical jobs.

In *Anarchism: a history of libertarian ideas* (Penguin 1986) George Woodcock discusses this survey and notes the preponderance of white-collar workers, and also of youth. "Anarchists in the 1940s had included a high proportion of the elderly, nostalgic moss-backed veterans, but of this batch in the 1960s, 65 per cent were under 40". He also notes the class shift. Of the over-sixties 45 per cent were working-class, as against 23 per cent in their thirties and 10 per cent in their twenties.

In 1993 *Freedom* did another readership survey. Of the first 100 respondents 79 called themselves anarchists. Of these 21 were anarcho-communists, 14 green anarchists, 7 anarchist-pacifists, 12 anarchist-syndicalists and 13 individualists. Only five were women. The largest age group was 19-40, 57 were in employment, and 43 per cent unemployed or retired. Professionals outnumbered manual workers 47 to 13. Their jobs included art teacher, language teacher, numerous librarians, journalists, an architect, a clinical psychologist, an osteopath and a "bank inspector". Analysis of the second 100 respondents told much the same story, though there were now 15 women.

This tells us something about the *Freedom* readership, but I repeat that *Freedom* is not representative, and some comrades would repeat this more loudly. Trying to say what anarchism is, and who is or is not an anarchist, is like trying to catch water in a net. Unless you're the police, a politician or the press, all of whom are clear in their own minds about who is an anarchist.

The man accused of being the Unabomber, for example, fits perfectly the clichéd preconceived idea of an anarchist. He has a beard, throws bombs and seems to have had a Thoreau-like life-style, rejecting technology, living in a Walden-style shack, far from anyone, without electricity or mains water, and with no other means of transport than a planet-friendly bicycle. Also, over a period of 17 years he delivered (though not by bicycle) 16 bombs, killing three people and injuring more than 20 others. A lone nutter with a beard — an Identikit anarchist if ever there was one, and the police, press and public immediately dubbed him as such.

Not so the anarchists. At the London Anarchist Book Fair in October (1996) leaflets were being distributed on behalf of the Ted Kaczynski Defence Campaign, which thinks he is innocent and was framed by the FBI. A different line is taken by *Freedom*. Its front page of April 20 is shared between two stories. One is headlined TONY BLAIR: Jesus Christ or Pontius Pilate?, the other THE UNABOMBER: IS HE AN ANARCHIST? The answer to the Tony Blair question is pretty obvious, but how would the ball bounce on the Unabomber? *Freedom* is somehow against war without being pacifist, and does not always condemn violence. When in apartheid South Africa President Verwoerd narrowly escaped an assassination attempt, *Freedom's* memorable headline read A PITY HE MISSED. This was what a lot of people thought; only *Freedom* lacked the hypocrisy not to say it out loud.

"Anarchists," *Freedom's* comment on the Unabomber begins, "are by definition opposed to people dominating other people by means of threats... The term 'anarchist' is often misapplied to mean anyone who uses illegal, secretive, violent means in pursuit of any social objective, however authoritarian." In the Unabomber's long-winded 232-page manifesto he denounces technology but, *Freedom* points out, he uses it. He rides a bicycle, which is a triumph of industrial technology. He uses sophisticated electrical technology to make his bombs, and he moves his explosive devices around the USA by forms of transport rather more sophisticated than a push-bike. "Some anarchists have used bombs, but most would rather remain unheard than kill people to gain attention. The majority of murderous fanatics are authoritarians." The Unabomber says in his ramblings that it is technology he is against, not governments. So, *Freedom* thunders, Theodore Kazcinsky is not an anarchist.

A mirror-image of the Unabomber case is that of William Morris. In 1984 there was a seminar at the Institute of Contemporary Arts celebrating Morris's 150th birthday. Tony Benn and Raymond Williams both puffed their pipes and lauded Morris as a socialist. Tony Benn got a good laugh when he said Mrs Thatcher had claimed Morris as an example of a 19th-century entrepreneur. A member of the audience made myself unpopular by saying that just for once Mrs T could be right. You could indeed argue that the wealthy entrepreneur who founded Morris & Co, Fine Art Workmen in Painting, Carving, Furniture and the Metals was a capitalist. Or you could plausibly argue that the author of *A Dream of John Ball* and *News From Nowhere* was an anarchist. In that visionary book he envisaged a society "which does not know the meaning of the words rich and poor, or the rights of property, or law." In *Nowhere* the Houses of Parliament have become a dung market. The narrator's guide, Old Hammond, tells him that in the old days Parliament was "a kind of watch-committee sitting to see the interests of the Upper Classes took no hurt."

Had he lived on, Morris might have recognised the socialism of G.D.H. Cole's Guild Socialism (anarcho-syndicalism, in effect) but it is hard to imagine that Morris would have had much time for Fabianism or the Labour

Party or for the centralised, dirigiste and nationalise-everything-in-sight state socialism as understood by Benn, Williams, Old Labour, Marxists and ex-Marxists (E.P. Thompson at one time appeared to claim Morris for Marxism).

Like Wilde, Morris loathed violence and distanced himself from the anarchists in the Socialist League. In return the anarchists ousted him from the editorship of *Commonweal* (of which he happened to be the proprietor and publisher). He was interested in Utopian commmunities, he had read Thoreau's *Walden* and Kropotkin's *The Conquest of Bread* and *Fields, Factories and Workshops*. He addressed Freedom Press meetings and spoke warmly of his "anarchist friends." These included Kropotkin, who attended his funeral. When you add to all this the drift of Morris's writings, his anarchist credentials look pretty good. Engels called him a "puppet" of the anarchists, which is quite a sound testimonial. (Proudhon called Marx the tapeworm of socialism.)

That ICA meeting was 13 years ago. The situation now is even more unreal. The Blairite New Labour has ditched Clause IV and is busily distancing itself from anything that smacks of socialism. At the same time they claim Morris as one of them. Never mind what he said, just feel the wallpaper. There's thus a rather droll squabble with Old Labour (or what's left of it) and New Labour both claiming Morris as theirs, when he wasn't Labour at all since he died before the Labour Party was formed, and wouldn't have liked them if he'd had the chance. Here's an irony. The anarchist Colin Ward's "News From Nowhere" column was the best thing in the old *New Statesman*. The new *New Statesman* has dispensed with Ward but retained the name of the column.

The examples of the Unabomber and William Morris show one thing clearly. This is that if someone is, in common parlance, a bad guy (like the Unabomber) then he's an anarchist. If he's a good guy (like William Morris) then he's not an anarchist but one of us ("us" extending way to the right of centre, beyond even the *New Statesman* to Thatcherdom itself).

Anarchists have always been divided on the issue of violence. Historically there have been those who went in for Propaganda of the Deed and those who preferred Propaganda of the Word. Propaganda of the Deed can take the form of nineteenth-century bomb-throwing assassination, armed struggle (the barricades of the Paris Commune, the Zapatistas, the Spanish Civil War) or it can be non-violent Direct Action, as with the Committee of 100, obstruction of by-pass building or refusal to pay the Poll Tax or demonstrating against the Criminal Justice Bill.

Michael Bakunin (1814-1876) was very much a Deed man, while at the same time being a prolific spouter of the Word. "From each according to his abilities, to each according to his needs": thus Bakunin in the declaration signed by 47 anarchists on trial after the Lyon uprising of 1870. (Marx took over the slogan in his *Criticism of the Gotha Programme* five years later.) Bakunin was huge in every sense, a heroic, romantic figure who would hurl himself into any revolution going and ask questions afterwards. His best-remembered saying (a paradox, naturally) is that "The urge for destruction is a creative urge." He started at an early age by inciting his brothers and sisters to rebel against their autocratic father, the owner of 500 serfs. In 1848 he rushed to Paris to join the revolution there, and in the same year he was manning the barricades in Prague. In 1849 he was in the thick of the Dresden insurrection. His heroics against the Prussian army so impressed the conductor of the Dresden Opera, Richard Wagner, that (according to G.B.Shaw) Siegfried was modelled on Bakunin. He was arrested and imprisoned in solitary confinement for eight years, during which time he had scurvy and all his teeth dropped out. Eventually he made a dramatic round-the-world escape from Siberia.

Proudhon's mutualist ideas were taken up by the First International Working Men's Association which included many of the Paris Communards (including Courbet: anarchist French painters of the period also include Pissarro, Signac, Steinlen and, later, Vlaminck). The IWMA also included Marx and Engels — and Bakunin. The resulting combination was explosive. It destroyed the First International, but it was a Bakunin-style act of creative destruction. Anarchism and communism had so far been practically synonymous. Bakunin split them apart and revealed the important difference.

It was almost incidental that in the process Bakunin exposed not only the authoritarianism of Marx's own personality but also the authoritarianism intrinsic to Marxism. Bakunin explained,

> I am not Communist, because Communism unites all forces of society in the State and becomes absorbed in it, because it inevitably leads to the concentration of all property in the hands of the State, while I seek the abolition of the State — the complete elimination of the principle of authority and governmental guardianship which, under the pretence of making men moral and civilising them, has up to now always enslaved, oppressed, exploited and ruined them.

The prophetic truth of his words has been borne out in this century in the Soviet Union and other countries which have followed the Marxist path or had it imposed on them.

In contrast to Bakunin's destructiveness was the constructive approach of Peter Kropotkin (1842-1917). He didn't want to replace capitalism with state ownership but by a system of co-operation, community and what he called (in the title of his best-known book) *Mutual Aid*, which was a counter-blast to social Darwinism. After years in exile Kropotkin returned to Russia in 1917 but quickly clashed with Lenin and the Bolsheviks. When he died in 1921 the procession of mourners in Moscow stretched for five miles, with anarchist banners bearing the words "Where there is authority there is no freedom".

Kropotkin's funeral was the last public anarchist manifestation in Soviet Russia. Nestor Makhno's anarchist army had twice saved the Bolshevik revolution from the old regime White Army (credit for which is routinely given to Trotsky). When the anarchist army had done the job and saved the Bolshevik bacon, Lenin and Trotsky crushed it ruthlessly and set about the systematic liquidation of anarchism, a policy that was energetically followed by Stalin. The predictions of Bakunin, Kropotkin and other anarchists were all proved right by the Russian revolution. The slogan "All power to the soviets" turned into "All power to the Supreme Soviet." In the USSR, and later elsewhere, Marxism led to totalitarian dictatorship. George Orwell was ambivalent about anarchism, calling himself a libertarian socialist, but in *Animal Farm* and *1984* he showed that the anarchist analysis had been right.

Kropotkin was a gentle man, universally loved and admired. Unfortunately he supported the Allies in the First World War. This was an aberration. Anarchists differ about all sorts of things, but they are against war. "War is the health of the State" is another classic anarchist paradox (first enunciated by Randolph Bourne). Its truth is apparent after only a moment's reflection. It is self-evident that the State is strongest in war-time, and the rights of the individual are weakest.

War is also the health of anarchism in so far as revulsion against militarism has led so many to an anarchist position. Tolstoy and Kropotkin both reacted against their military backgrounds. Thoreau's civil disobedience came from rejecting the Mexican war. The Aldermaston marches produced many pacifists and anarchists and the Committee of 100. Its best-known member was Bertrand Russell, whose mighty intellect was not always consistent but for most of the time was of a distinctly anarchist bent. And the anarchist sympathies of the almost equally brainy Noam Chomsky were roused by the Vietnam war.

There have been thousands of others, less well-known, who have followed Fritzhof Nansen's words: "Wars will cease when men refuse to fight." They often did so at the cost of their lives. Such a one was Olaf. The anarchist poet e.e.cummings was so egalitarian that he did his best to dispense even with capital letters. Olaf was an honourable exception:

> i sing of Olaf glad and big
> whose warmest heart recoiled at war:
> a conscientious object-or

His "wellbeloved colonel"

> (westpointer most succinctly bred)
> took erring Olaf soon in hand

For refusing to become a soldier Olaf is horribly tortured but ("without getting annoyed") he continues to repeat the words, "I will not kiss your fucking flag." As he is finally tortured to death

> Olaf (upon what once were knees)
> does almost ceaselessly repeat
> "there is some shit I will not eat."

Olaf was a First World War conscientious objector. Vernon Richards was a conscientious objector in the Second. Now in his early eighties (and looking as though he is in his early sixties) Richards has long been a key figure in the anarchist scene. His father, Emilio Recchioni, was an Italian anarchist who spent five years in exile on Mediterranean islands which were brutal places then and are now holiday resorts. He came to London as a political refugee — as had Marat, Marx, Bakunin, Herzen, Malatesta, Trotsky and so many others before him (not so easy with Home Secretary Michael Howard). He joined the Italian community in Soho and in due course acquired King Bomba, the

Italian food shop (trademark "The Sole Macaroni Factory In England") that used to be a Soho landmark at 37 Old Compton Street. The name King Bomba has no anarchist connotation: it is the nickname of King Ferdinand IV of Naples, Ferdinand III of Sicily and Ferdinand I of the Two Sicilies (all one person).

His son Vernon (Vero to his friends, and Recchioni having become Richards) learnt the violin. This, with growing up in the food shop, had the ingredients of a good education according to the recipe of the sort-of anarchist Charles Fourier — cookery and music. More formally he went on to study civil engineering at King's College London. One aspect of anarchism is freedom from specialisation, and as well as working as a civil engineer on the Great Western Railway, he has been a travel courier, a grocer at King Bomba's and for the last 28 years an organic farmer and market gardener on one hectare of land in Essex. He isn't physically as active as he used to be but he produces about 500 pounds of aubergines, peppers and zucchini a year, and plenty of fruit. At 82 he still does a 22-mile newspaper round on Sundays, bringing (as he says) "the bad news" to 70 customers. And for as long as anyone can remember he has tirelessly contributed to and kept going the Freedom Press.

One of his many careers has been as a photographer. He took the most famous photograph of Orwell, the one that is on the cover of most of Orwell's books. On VE day May 1945 a French magazine got him to photograph Orwell, Herbert Read, Stephen Spender and George Woodcock. "You couldn't imagine a more dreary bunch. Orwell was very nice but not very communicative. Herbert Read was very nice too, but I never spoke to him again after his knighthood." The anarchist Read's acceptance of a knighthood is indeed hard to explain or excuse.

First with a Brownie Box camera, later with a Leica, Richards photographed in his free moments, always doing his own darkroom work. A selection has recently been published in *A Weekend Photographer's Notebook* (Freedom Press, a bargain at £6.95). They are reminiscent of the Golden Age (or, rather, black-and-white) of *Picture Post,* and contain memorable scenes of London, Paris and Spain over a period of 40 years or so.

The Spanish Civil War prompted Richards in 1936 to edit *Spain and The World* and to reactivate the Freedom Press. This was succeeded by *Revolt!* in 1939, and then *War Commentary* which resulted in 1944 in the arrest and imprisonment of Richards and his co-editors Dr John Hewetson and Philip Sansom for spreading disaffection in the army. The fascinating, sometimes comic story of this episode is worth looking up. The paper's cartoonist John Olday was sentenced to twelve months for "stealing by finding an identity card"; Philip Sansom had already been imprisoned "for being in possession of an army waterproof coat and for failing to notify a change of address." The authorities had nothing to fear from the minute number of anarchists, but they cracked down hard, thereby winning the anarchists the public support of George Orwell, Herbert Read, Harold Laski, Kingsley Martin, Benjamin Britten, Augustus John and Bertrand Russell, with the *New Statesman* denouncing "spiteful prosecutions".

One member of the armed forces who had received Freedom Press literature was George Melly, who had been conscripted into the Royal Navy at the end of the war. The idea of George Melly in Jack-Tar uniform with bell-bottom trousers makes it hardly surprising that he became an anarchist of the surrealist persuasion. In *Rum, Bum and Concertina* he tells of his discovery of anarchism: "What a beautiful concept! A rational world in which what you made was for use not profit, and all you took was what you needed. Love was the only law. Money unnecessary. Crime, once envy, greed, and private possessions no longer existed, would be unnecessary. Why steal when you could take freely? Free sexuality." Melly openly displayed quantities of Freedom Press pamphlets, including works by Bakunin, Kropotkin, George Woodcock and Herbert Read, and was had up on a charge. He astutely defended himself by showing that his reading matter contained nothing that wasn't to be found in the works of George Bernard Shaw which were freely available in the ship's library.

Another conscript found in possession of Freedom Press literature was Colin Ward. Born in Wanstead, Essex, in 1924, he left school at 15 to work in the Council housing department, and then as an architectural draughtsman. He was called up in 1942 and didn't get out till 1947. He would have been demobilised sooner, had Sapper Ward, number 1439275, not been required to spend 56 days behind bars for what he calls "some act of bloody-mindedness." Because of possessing the Freedom Press literature, he was called as a prosecution witness in the *War Commentary* trial. He and the other conscripts were asked "Have you been seduced from your duty?" Naturally they all said No, except for "some conscientious Christian git" who said Yes.

After demob Ward was asked to join the *Freedom* editorial group. He was one of the editors from 1947-60. For the next 10 years he edited the exceptionally informative and thoughtful monthly *Anarchy*. By way of a day job he was an architectural draughtsman for about ten years, then spent a year getting teaching qualifications. He taught Liberal Studies at Wandsworth, and then for eight years edited *BEE* (the Bulletin of Environmental Education). He was also education officer of the Town and Country Planning Association. He has been showered with Honorary Doctorates all over the place, and this year the boy who left school at 15 was the Visiting Centennial Professor, Department of Social Policy at the London School of Economics.

He has written umpteen books, on subjects that range from vandalism to housing, the child in the city, the child in the country, work, water ... there are too many to list. His Penguin on *Education* has gone through seven editions; *Anarchy in Action* has been translated into ten languages. He is especially interesting when writing about such subjects as allotments and holiday camps about which so many people are so damned condescending.

A particularly beguiling book of his is on *Chartres* (Folio Society)*. Though he has long architectural experience this might seem at first sight a surprising subject for the non-Christian Ward but he takes an interesting anarchist spin on it. He points out that Chartres Cathedral is not the work of a single genius but of thousands of people. And it is a mess. The first thing you notice about the West front is its lack of symmetry. It is a breath-takingly beautiful mess, but a mess all the same. It is the work of anonymous people, and it is something that has grown rather than been planned.

Ward has edited Kroptkin and is Kropotkin's greatest exponent and follower. Here's an example of Ward's approach. In *Anarchy in Action*, (1973) he mentions how Kropotkin gave lifeboat institutions as an example of voluntary mutual aid without top-down authority. Ward comments:

> Two other examples which we often use to help people to conceive the federal principle which anarchists see as the way in which local groups and associations could combine for complex functions without any central authority are the postal service and the railways. You can post a letter from here to China or Chile, confident that it will arrive, as a result of freely arrived-at agreements between different national post offices, without there being any central postal authority at all. Or you can travel across Europe over the lines of a dozen railway systems — capitalist and communist — co-ordinated by agreement between different railway undertakings, without any kind of central railway authority.

―――――――――――
Chartres will be re-issued by Five Leaves Publications in 1997.

Ward has acted like a yeast, the fermenting agent of ideas in the minds of countless others. His influence in areas from housing to teaching and planning has been immense, and will continue to grow. Reviewing Ward's latest book in the *Times Literary Supplement* Nicolas Walter gives a good summary:

> The message throughout is the same as in all Ward's work for half a century. It is a pragmatic form of anarchism, seen as a theory of organisation, a combination of self-help and mutual aid, of do-it-yourself and do-it-together. Ward is calling not so much for a political revolution as for social transformation — though not all that much of one, since he sees anarchism all around us, and likes to find examples wherever ordinary people put freedom into practice in their daily lives. His anarchism is not deductive, drawn down from a general ideology to particular instances, but inductive, drawn up from a mass of instances to a principle of action.

The name of Nicolas Walter (frequently mis-spelt) will be known to readers of many journals as a prolific writer of letters to the editor. Born in Bristol in 1934, son of the neurologist Grey Walter, he spent his national service on the Russian language course in the RAF. He was at Oxford when the New Left was emerging, and an early published letter was to the *Manchester Guardian* at the time of the Hungary uprising and Suez invasion 40 years ago (it was to be seen in the facsimile pages of the *Guardian's* 150th anniversary issue).

This letter led Colin Ward to send Walter a copy of *Freedom*. He heard Philip Sansom (a great orator) at Speaker's Corner, and gradually realised that his position was an anarchist one. He has worked in teaching and publishing and for seven years was chief sub-editor of the *Times Lit-*

erary Supplement (succeeding, as it happens, me). Since 1974 he has been director of the Rationalist Press Association. He was a founder member of the Committee of 100 in 1960, and in 1963 was involved in the Spies for Peace, who so spectacularly published the whereabouts of the RSGs. These were Regional Seats of Government, consisting of underground bunkers in which in the event of nuclear war the government could live on — presumably with the personal responsibility of propagating the human race when the rest of us got blown up. The existence of the RSGs was Top Secret until the Spies for Peace came along, pin-pointing their whereabouts for good measure.

Walter was also involved with the Vietnam Action Group in 1966, and he got two months in prison for demonstrating against Harold Wilson in a Brighton Church. He has written countless historical and polemical articles and tirelessly promotes a secular view against religious ones, whether of a hard fundamentalist nature or the Prayer For The Day milk-and-water kind.

Sadly Walter is confined to a wheelchair now, but his mind is as active as ever, as he has shown in the events following the death of Albert Isadore Meltzer who collapsed and died at the age of 76 at an anarcho-syndcalist conference in May.

Meltzer fitted the popular idea of an anarchist, but the press portrayed him not as a dangerous figure but as a comic one, almost cuddly. He was described as larger than life (and he was indeed a big man), as "one of the most cherished figureheads of the anarchist movement", as "one of the most enduring and respected torchbearers of the international anarchist movement in the second half of the twentieth century" and "a remarkably gentle, generous and gracious soul".

He had been a boxer, ran armaments to Spain during the civil war, and played a part in the Cairo mutiny after the war; he had been a fairground promoter, a theatre-hand, a second-hand bookseller and a *Daily Telegraph* copytaker. At his funeral his hearse was drawn by plumed horses, there was a stand-up comedian at the crematorium; there was a home video of the deceased laughing, and the coffin went into the incinerator to the strains of Marlene Dietrich.

Meltzer's obituary in the *Guardian* was signed by Stuart Christie. Newspapers in the Seventies habitually referred to Christie as "Britain's best-known anarchist". He had got himself a term in a Spanish jail for his part in an inept plot to bump off Franco. Christie is from Scotland and the story had it that, when he was arrested, the explosives were under his kilt and in his sporran. This wasn't literally true, but he was conspicuous enough for the *Guardia Civil* to spot him pretty quickly. After returning to Britain he spent 16 months on remand in Brixton at the time of the Angry Brigade business, and was acquitted.

Christie's *Guardian* obituary says that Meltzer was "a torchbearer for the international anarchist movement". "While a gentle, generous and gracious soul, his championship of anarchism as a revolutionary working class movement led to conflict with the neo-liberals who dominated the movement in the late 1940s. Many otherwise politically incompatible people were drawn to anarchism because of its militant tolerance." (Militant tolerance? A curious phrase).

The subsequent obituaries in the *Times* and *Telegraph* take a similar line about how Albert was "vehemently opposed to the re-packaging and marketing of anarchism as a broad church for academia-orientated quietists and single-issue pressure groups" and "academia-orientated liberals and pacifists spawned by the disillusionment of war."

Much of this rhetoric is similar to that of Spiro Agnew denouncing the university campus opponents of the Vietnam war, but here the target of the not-so-coded language is the Freedom group. In the *Guardian* obituary Meltzer "brought countless young people into the anarchist movement". In the *Telegraph* he "was responsible for bringing so many people into the movement over the last 30 years."

In the *Times* — having come down from "countless young people" to "so many people" — Meltzer brings "several recruits into the movement". Several is probably about right.

The obituary in the *Independent* painted a rather different picture. Nicolas Walter said that Meltzer "saw himself as a protagonist of the militant working-class anarcho-syndicalist movement, something which had existed in many parts of the world when he began but which scarcely exists anywhere today." He goes on to say that Meltzer "broke with the moderates associated with the established Freedom Press, whom he described as academics and mandarins and denounced as liberals and pacifists (even 'non-violent fascists') and took a strongly militant — even militarist line."

Walter went on to tell how Meltzer had teamed up with Stuart Christie after Christie's release from prison in Spain and that "they were involved in the turn towards urban guerilla methods which appealed to frustrated revolutionaries, and culminated in this country in the Angry Brigade in the 1970s." He concluded by saying that Meltzer "was a large fund of good stories, which were often true. He could be a loyal and witty friend; he could also be a ruthless and bitter enemy. But he never gave up, and even his opponents respected his lifelong commitment to class struggle and libertarian revolution."

This was fair-minded, balanced and even generous, considering that Meltzer had subjected Walter and others in the Freedom group to a stream of libellous abuse for 30 years. Yet a few days later the *Independent's* obituary page carried what looked like a correction, saying that "Stuart Christie was acquitted of all charges relating to the activities of the Angry Brigade and Mr Meltzer was never considered a suspect by the police. We apologise for any imputation to the contrary."

Walter's obituary had made no such imputation. Why then was the *Independent* apologising? What had happened was that the *Independent* had received a letter from

B.M. Birnberg & Co, a firm of solicitors which has over many years earned an admirable reputation for its defence of civil liberties. Birnberg's letter demanded from the *Independent* a retraction, an apology, that they "indemnify our client in respect of his costs" and contribute £250 to a library that Meltzer was associated with. A copy of this letter was sent to Walter who replied to Birnberg expressing his disgust "that such a letter should be written by a so-called liberal lawyer on behalf of a so-called anarchist client." He added that the *Independent* had neither consulted or informed him before publishing its apology and that if it had been up to him his reaction would have been the same as that of the defendants in the case of Arkell v. Pressdram (i.e. *Private Eye*) — namely, Fuck off! He said the demands for money were beneath contempt and concluded by noting that, 30 years after he and Birnberg first met, Birnberg still couldn't spell Nicolas Walter's name.

Vernon Richards also joined in. His INSTEAD OF AN OBITUARY (*Freedom*, 16 May) starts by denouncing the "self-publicity and fantasy contained in (Meltzer's) recently published 400-page autobiography" and the "quite extraordinary and equally fantastic obituary by the erstwhile amateur 'terrorist' anarchist Stuart Christie". He quotes at length from the *Guardian* obit and then comments "But it just isn't true!"

He remembers that he and Meltzer went together to the Labour Exchange at the beginning of the Second World War to register as conscientious objectors. He derides claims for Meltzer's part in the Cairo Mutiny, and as for his "helping to organise arms shipments from Hamburg to Spain" and his being "a contact for the Spanish anarchist intelligence service" Richards says that "as I write I am bursting my sides with laughter!"

Richards fights some old battles. Contrary to the Christie version it was "neo-Liberals" who "actually defended and rescued Meltzer from the anarcho-syndicalists, who wanted to exclude him from the Anarchist Federation in 1940." He says Meltzer's "most virulent opponents were Tom Brown, Bill Gape and two others whose names escape me (one an Irishman who was found dead in Hyde Park, and a Scotsman — apologies for old age)." He recalls his last meeting with Meltzer on which occasion Richards told him that "though five years older than him, I would have the opportunity to write his obituary". Which, he concludes, "I have just done, and I admit WITH SADNESS (because after all we were comrades together for some twenty years) But I believe that for the past thirty years he did more harm than good to the anarchist cause".

If that was the bludgeon, the rapier followed (*Freedom*, June 8).

> ALBERT'S FUNERAL
>
> Albert Meltzer's funeral, on Friday 24th May, was a lavish affair paid for by himself, with a hearse drawn by two black horses, a marching jazz-band, a stand-up comedian... Some might say this was his final humorous act of self-aggrandisement, but it was also a contribution to anarchist propaganda — some might say his first for thirty years. 230 people, including many people with whom Albert had fallen out in his quarrelsome later life, walked through Lewisham in his funeral procession. It was reported in the national press, and excited some interest in anarchism as such. We agree with Albert that his passing should be celebrated with jollity.

The report is unsigned but is believed to be the work of the *Freedom* Wildcat cartoonist Donald Rooum.

This is all quite entertaining for the bystander, if not entirely comradely. What this personal squabbling does show is that the mass working-class movement dreamt of by Meltzer is a thing of the past. This is not at all the same as saying that anarchism has had its day. In one form or another it is widespread and vigorous. There may not be a mass movement but, as Colin Ward says, there is a mass of movements. Anarchists have been in the forefront of the environmental movement: Murray Bookchin's *Our Synthetic Environment* was published months before Rachel Carson's *The Silent Spring*, and is far more comprehensive and challenging. Anarchists have been active in the areas of animal rights, feminism, opposition to the Poll Tax and the Criminal Justice Bill. There are the activities of George Monbiot and the land campaign that occupied thirteen Guinness acres of Wandsworth. There are the motorway and by-pass objections and all sorts of other effective actions that take place without organised leadership or planning. (Since writing this we have seen the continuation and conclusion of the immense McLibel case). There isn't room to mention them all, and I am aware that in this headlong survey of the anarchist scene I have made glaring omissions, and also that much of what I have said will be found contentious. (*Note: It was! In the original article I said that Stuart Christie was at the Anarchist Book Fair. Apparently he wasn't, which I am prepared to accept, though I'm puzzled as to why the suggestion was so offensive. A number of feminists objected to the omission of women from my account. I certainly should have found space for mention of Vernon Richards's partner Marie-Louise Berneri, who died tragically young, or Emma Goldman, whose autobiography* Living My Life *is well worth reading. But the relative absence of women from anarchist history is not something I can remedy, though the reasons for it would be well worth exploring*).

One further species of anarchist that must be mentioned are those who (without waiting for the revolution) have found an anarchist solution in their own lives, somewhat in the way of the "internal exiles" in the old Soviet empire. Downshifting, working at home with new technology, being nearly self-sufficient in food, cutting living standards and improving the quality of life, earning less and enjoying more... in such ways many people have had their own revolution.

It has also been noticeable how quasi-anarchism keeps cropping up in the most respectable company. Will Hutton (October 6, 1996, *Observer*) mourned the way building societies and mutual insurance companies are becoming publicly quoted companies. He says that one of the great legacies of the nineteenth century is being squandered. These are "the financial institutions founded on the principle of collective self-help and mutual ownership... Mutuality is too precious an idea to die." It sounds like pure Kropotkin, or Colin Ward.

Or take Neal Ascherson (*IoS* September 22). He is discussing what will happen now Labour has dumped socialism, and speaks of "the conviction, a century older than Marxism, that the human race is a naturally co-operative species. The vision is of a small community of producers, human beings who live together without property or economic privileges and live in a harmony which springs from their dependence on one another. Only anarchists put this vision into practice."

And for my final witness I call Mr Tony Blair. Appalled at the low turn-out in elections he said he would rather people voted not necessarily for Labour but for any party rather than not vote at all. So, apparently, for Mr Blair it doesn't matter which direction you're going in as long as you follow a leader. Mr Blair unwittingly confirms what the anarchists have always said. "If voting changed anything, they wouldn't allow it". "Don't vote. It only encourages them". "If voting changed anything, they'd make it illegal".

In the General Election in May the turn-out was down.

The above first appeared, in a slightly different form, as Anarchy among the Anarchists in the Guardian, *16th November, 1996.*

THE CANDIDATE

Sir James Goldsmith's last public appearance was on that hectic General Election night in May, when he appeared to be barking. We did not know he was dying. Now, only a few months later, his name and fame seem to belong to a distant past — a reminder, at most, of the vanity of human wishes, a name "to point a moral and adorn a tale". It is worth remembering, though, before he is entirely forgotten, that it was from a Labour government that he received his knighthood, just as it should not be forgotten that Robert Maxwell (a greater and more detestable monster) had been a Labour MP.

How different (we fervently hope) is the brave New Labour world — but that remains a hope, and it is too soon to uncross the fingers. Realistically, the best we can hope for is that Tony Blair will prove a better Conservative Prime Minister than his predecessors. And, in all fairness, not having a Prime Minister Michael Howard or Michael Portillo is much to be thankful for.

If James Goldsmith is already becoming a dim memory, the European Parliamentary elections of 1994 are entirely forgotten. Until re-reading what I wrote at the time I had even forgotten that it was Sir James who prompted my involvement in that massively unimportant event. It is the knowledge that future historians will ignore it completely that boldens me to offer this contemporary account by a participant in what would otherwise have no memorial.

My campaign reports for a daily newspaper inevitably required a certain amount of repetition for the sake of readers who had missed earlier insalments. I have eliminated these as much as possible. Otherwise what appears is substantially in its original form and without benefit of hindsight.

March 29 1994

The other day Sir James Goldsmith announced that he's going to stand for the European Parliament. Someone asked me why I didn't do the same. What an extraordinary suggestion. It's not as though I'm in the habit of following where Sir James leads. On reflection, though, the idea seemed too daft to reject out of hand.

Sir David Steel managed to be a Euro-candidate in Italy, so my first thought was to stand in Guadeloupe or Martinique, which is where I have just got back from and wouldn't at all mind going back to. Guadeloupe and Martinique are technically part of France, and therefore part of Europe, whatever the atlas may say.

As soon as I started looking into the matter I found that the whole business is quite complicated enough already if I just stick to my home patch without going to the trouble and expense of crossing the ocean for an away match.

First I've got to get £1,000 for the deposit. Sir James has the edge over me here. He is reported to have £800 million. I am reputed to have less than that. Incidentally, why is the deposit £1,000 when it's £500 to stand for Westminster?

Then I have to get the signatures of a proposer and a seconder, and of 28 electors registered in the constituency with their electoral numbers (see Note 3). Note 3 is on a form called ELECTION OF A MEMBER Cat.No.EP4 which by its casual use of pronouns shows it assumes that a person is male. Furthermore it includes the word "parliamenmtary" and omits the apostrophe in "electors' lists". Be that as it may, I can foresee a few congenial evenings in the pub collecting the autographs of 30 electors. This would be less easy in Martinique because 1. I don't know any registered electors there, 2. Martinique politics are incomprehensible to an outsider and highly volatile at the moment and 3. There are no pubs in Martinique.

When shortly after closing time I mentioned my signature-collecting plan, Mr Knowall (who dilutes his Scotch with whisky) said I wouldn't be able to collect signatures in the pub because it could be construed as buying votes and would therefore be an offence under the Representation of the People Act of 1066. This sounded like good news because it would rule out buying drinks for 30 pub regulars (starting with Mr Knowall) until after the election, but my local Returning Officer didn't think that buying a drink was something that would bother him a lot, especially since signing a nomination paper doesn't necessarily mean that you're going to vote for a person. So there, Mr Knowall. Same again?

I have just mentioned my local Returning Officer but here again we have a problem. Who *is* my Returning Officer? What is my constituency? At a General Election my constituency would be (is) Newbury, but for matters concerning Euro elections the Newbury Returning Officer referred me to his opposite number in the Vale of White Horse in Abingdon, Oxfordshire. White Horse explained that my Euro seat was Hampshire North and Oxford, or would be as soon as the French (there we go again, blame the French) signed something or other. Until such time I am in Wiltshire. I was about to express surprise that my constituency was Hampshire, Oxfordshire or Wiltshire when I live in Berkshire, but remembering that Martinique is in Europe I decided not to bother.

In search of my constituency I then got on to the United Kingdom Information Office of the European Parliament, who put me on to the Home Office who referred me to the Foreign Office who referred me back to the Home Office who referred me to my local Returning Officer who said (a few days having passed by now) that he still didn't know whether I was in Hampshire North and Oxford or in Wiltshire. Finally a frightfully helpful chap at the Home Office was able to refer me to Commands 2440 and 2441 which make it clear that in this neck of Berkshire we are definitely in Hampshire North and Oxford. Or will be when the French have signed their bit of paper.

Having got that far, I felt that not standing in Martinique had been one of my better ideas.

Ideas, yes ideas. Must have some ideas, possibly even an ideology. These are essential ingredients for a manifesto. Policies too. I've got to write a manifesto. What shall I offer the electorate?

One of my political heroes is the old Latin Quarter character Ferdinand Lop. In the days of the Fourth Republic, when there was a new Government every week, Lop used to stand for election whenever possible, a Gallic prototype of Screaming Lord Sutch. I remember only one of his policies, which was that the Boulevard Saint-Michel should be extended in both directions until it reached the sea. Whenever there was a political crisis Lop would go to the Brasserie Lipp and sit by the phone waiting for the call from the Elysée asking him to form a government. Eventually a party was formed in opposition to Lop. They called themselves — naturally — anti-Lops.

In honour of the great man I will put his Boul'Mich extension scheme at the top of my agenda. What else can I offer the voters? Bread and circuses. No taxation without representation. Give us back our eleven days. Abolish VAT. Tax traffic cones.

There's a good bit in *Sylvie and Bruno*, the Lewis Carroll book that hardly anyone reads. In the course of an insurrection a crowd forms outside the palace, and what they are all chanting is "LESS BREAD! MORE TAXES!" That should get me a few votes. Or not.

Perhaps I should take a few leaves out of the Icelandic book. In that amazing country they have no television broadcasting during daylight hours, which means none at all in the summer months, and — this is brilliant — every member of Parliament is required to make a speech in rhyming verse once a year.

I propose that all old-age pensioners should be given a free bottle of whisky (or alcoholic equivalent) every week. This would create employment in the drinks trade and in the distributive one. Instead of a milkman you would have a Scotchman in a kilt clinking his bottles on the doorstep in the early hours and saying "Och aye the noo'." Or if you preferred Irish whiskey it would be "Top of the morning, sor or mam, would it be the Teachers, the Bushmills or the Paddy you'll be after having?" Simple pleasures, and not expensive. The old folks would be much better off with a sound nightcap than with tranquilisers (my GP actually agrees on this one) and if the OAPs are teetotal then they will soon find that their accumulating bottles have won them plenty of new friends and acquaintances who are just dropping by, thereby relieving the social services.

Here's another idea. Look at what the Tories have done; then reverse it. What was the first action for which Margaret Thatcher is remembered? Depriving children of their free milk. What was the first thing that Edward Heath tried to do when he became Prime Minister? Introduce museum charges. And so on. I would give back the milk to the kids, and I wouldn't just abolish museum charges; I'd pay people to go to museums and libraries and plays and films and concerts. Pour money into art schools and rail transport, abolish the armed forces, the civil service, school exams and Greenwich Mean Time.

I am the first to admit that my manifesto needs working on. It requires more than just a little fine-tuning. I would welcome suggestions from readers. Come to think of it, how about standing as candidate for the Guardian Letter-Writers' Party? What was that you just said, yes, you at the back of the class? I thought that's what you said and the answer is No. I will not be standing for the Boston Tea Party.

On second thoughts it's not such a bad idea. No taxation without representation.

April 5

In a major after-dinner speech after dinner last night I gave a comprehensive update report and general overview of the progress of my candidacy in the imminent elections for the European Parliament. I announced that I would be running on a dream ticket alliance of the Vole Party and the Campaign for Real Life, under the umbrella title of the Boston Tea Party. This took the assembled company completely by surprise. Both of them interpreted this as an important policy reversal. One of them went so far as to call it a U-turn.

I reiterated that politicians had to be prepared to take rough knocks and added "I have got a programme. I believe in that programme. I am not going to be knocked off it." Funnily enough the Prime Minister, in a Major speech, used precisely the same words the next day.

In a departure from my prepared speech I repeated my reluctant decision not to stand in Martinique or Guadeloupe. This announcement has caused widespread disappointment among the populations of these beautiful (and non-cricket-playing) Caribbean islands. Other far-flung European islands where I will also not be a candidate include Réunion, Madeira, the Canaries and the Azores.

Perhaps I'll get round to one of these places in the next lot of elections, which will be in 1999. Meanwhile I'm having my work cut out to get my nomination in on time right here in Berkshire. And time is quickly running out. Nomination papers have to be delivered to the Returning Officer by May 12. Not later than 4 pm, it specifies on the form. And I still don't know whether I am standing in Wiltshire or in Hampshire North and Oxford. The last time I spoke to the Home Office they were quite confident that Newbury (my constituency for the Westminster parliament) will be in Hampshire North and Oxford.

Anyway, by not later than 4pm on May 12th I have to have 30 signatures of registered electors in whatever constituency it is that I am standing in. I have been able to establish one thing at least, and this is that whether it's the old Euro-constituency (Wiltshire) or the new one (Hampshire North and Oxford) it will include Newbury District (which is in Berkshire). This means that (and do pay attention because it's a bit complicated and I'm only going to say it once) at present the only way I can be sure of getting signatures that are valid is by getting those of electors registered in the Newbury District area. I also have to get their Electoral Numbers.

To find the electoral numbers I have to get hold of a copy of the electoral register. The electoral register is just a list of names, addresses and numbers. It shouldn't be any bigger or more expensive to produce than a telephone directory for the same area. So how much do you think a set of electoral registers for the District of Newbury would cost? Make a guess. Think of a large sum. Double it. Double it again. You are still nowhere near. A set of the registers of electors for the District of Newbury costs £440. And Newbury is only about a third or quarter of the Euro-constituency.

Now for Catch-22. When you've collected your 30 signatures and your nomination has been accepted and you're a qualified candidate, then you are entitled for (wait for it) a FREE COPY OF THE ELECTORAL REGISTER. At precisely the moment when you no longer have need of it. It must have taken some ingenuity to think that one up.

In spite of all these obstacles I have already managed to acquire most of the signatures necessary. Collecting the electoral numbers to go with them is a bridge I will have to cross when I come to it.

The form starts off as follows; "We, the undersigned, being electors for the said Constituency, do hereby nominate the under-mentioned person as a candidate for the said election."

As the under-mentioned person I have to fill in four little boxes. Three are easy — Home address in full, Candidate's surname, Other names in full. But then there's a box headed Description. How should I describe myself? I've been asking for suggestions. Here are some of the replies. White male, bald with glasses. Shifty. Daft.

I don't like any of these. One of Her Majesty's Inspectors of Taxes once described me (to my cost) as "Recklessly

Negligent" but I don't think that would look very good on a nomination paper. I think I'll go along with the girl from Ipanema — "Tall and tanned and young and lovely."

My next exhibit comes from Her Majesty's Stationery Office. It is called European Parliamentary Elections Act 1993, and it is very pertinent (and probably also germane) to the issue because it is "An Act to give effect to a Decision of the Council of the European Communities, 93/81/Euratom, ECSC, EEC, of 1st February 1993 having the effect of increasing the number of United Kingdom representatives to be elected to the European Parliament; and for connected purposes".

What are connected purposes? It doesn't matter; let's get on with the story.

Now comes a letter B which is half an inch high and introduces us to ringing words which should be accompanied by the sound of trumpets: "BE IT ENACTED, by the Queen's most Excellent Majesty, by and with the advice and consent of the Lords Spiritual and Temporal, and Commons..."

After this stirring build-up it is a bit of a let-down to find all that is being said by the Lords Spiritual and Temporal, and Commons, is such things as that in the European Parliamentary Act 1978 for "81" there shall be substituted "87".

This is actually of immediate relevance to me because it concerns how many Euro-constituencies we are going to have and therefore whether my bit of Berkshire is in Hampshire, Wiltshire or Oxford. The other point of interest is that this document, which consists of just one piece of paper, costs no less than £1.50.

In my next report I hope to be able to tell you how much an MEP earns. I have an idea that it's quite a lot. In his entertaining memoirs Roy Jenkins says his salary in Brussels was "apparently high (by the standards of the 1970s)". £50,000. Supplemented by allowances of £15,000 to £20,000. He comments that "The position was obviously more than tolerable." It is because I am in search of just such a more than tolerable situation that I will soon be appealing for votes in whatever constituency it turns out I am standing in.

April 13

There's no point in trying to disguise the fact that what happened on Saturday was a disaster. Unmitigated. In the past Mr Boston has proved reliable. The season before last I started with a fiver. By consistently and judiciously backing Mr Boston I ended up with nearly thirty quid. Last season wasn't quite so good. In fact it turned the thirty quid back into a fiver. Even so.

Mr Boston is the only horse I ever back. Imagine, then, my excitement on finding that he was running in the Grand National. My confidence was reinforced by what Chris Hawkins said in the pages of the *Guardian*. "My best long shot is Mr Boston, a thorough stayer with some form on the soft." I naturally got down to the Turf Accountant pretty sharpish and invested the entire campaign funds of the Boston Tea Party. This meant a fiver each way at 18 to 1.

He fell at the thirteenth.

On reflection it was perhaps an exaggeration to call this an unmitigated disaster. It is often just such a set-back that spurs one on to even greater efforts, especially if one is a thorough stayer with some form on the soft. The financial setback, however, makes it more essential than ever that I should be elected to the European Parliament and thereby receive the fabulous remuneration.

I've had a bit of a job finding out just how vast this lolly is because the Press Offices and Information Offices of Whitehall, Brussels and Strasbourg work very short hours indeed, and they take immensely long weekends. In Whitehall they don't just have Good Friday and Easter Monday off but Maundy Thursday as well. Whenever I phone with an inquiry I find myself talking to the security officer.

They're fine people, security officers. They're polite, good-humoured, work round the clock and never take time off. They are also well-informed. One of them even told me how much a Euro-MP earns. He said it was the same as a Westminster MP, adding (with emphasis) *"Plus allowances"*. It turns out that he was perfectly correct. An MEP gets £31,687 per annum. But that's just the start of it. They get a travel rate allowance of 57p per kilometre for the first 800 km and 29p for each additional kilometre for travel within the Community to attend official meetings.

In Hansard of February 15 Mr Heathcoat-Amory states that "Members are reimbursed the actual cost of the return air fare by the most direct route for travel outside the EC to attend official meetings." I like the phrase "the actual cost". And they receive up to £2,340 per annum for travel on official business other than to attend official meetings.

It gets better. Subsistence allowance of 199 ECU (approx £155) per day (repeat, per day) for attending official meetings within the European Community *plus* the cost of overnight accommodation. Secretarial assistance of up to £5,826 per month. General Expenditure Allowance of £2,131 per month for office management costs, telephone. This is halved in respect of Members who, "for no valid reason", have failed to attend at least half the number of plenary sittings. And a Data Processing allowance of £780 per annum for purchase or rent of equipment. This last figure strikes me as paltry. Otherwise it all sounds very jolly. In fact I feel more and more that I WANT THE JOB.

The Hansard entry which immediately precedes the one from which I have gleaned this information gives a further insight into Euro-accountancy. It goes like this:

> Mr. Nelson (pursuant to his answer, 17 December 1993, column 977): The total figure given for the European Investment Bank's subscribed capital was 57.6 million ecu, while

the limit on the banks total outstanding lending was given as 144 million ecu. These figures are incorrect, and should have read 57.6 billion ecu and 144 billion ecu respectively.

This shows what we're up against. We're up against people who get their millions mixed up with their billions.

When I'm an MEP I will have a huge office staff and everything will run like a Swiss watch, if that's not an inappropriate simile. If it is inappropriate then, frankly my dear, I don't give a damn. However, until that time when I have all this dosh to pay menials to do my work for me I have these piles of paper all over the place. Among them, unaided by 25 grand a year of office assistance, I have managed to find the piece of paper which tells me (and now you) that Jacques Delors, aged 68, has a salary of £167,548. Plus expenses. Chauffeur driven car, pension.

Actually I think Jacques Delors is rather a good egg but the next exhibit isn't about eggs but fish. In the Common Market (or European Community, as we must learn to call it) there is only one kind of fish. It is called "Cod Equivalent". In negotiations all fish are cod. Or Cod Equivalent. Thus, one cod equals six mackerel.

A couple of weeks ago there was a meeting in Brussels which ended at three in the morning. Afterwards Theodoros Pangalos, the Greek Deputy Foreign Minister who had chaired the meeting, said "We spent six hours discussing 1,100 tons of cod, which cost $220,000." Which is, I suppose, roughly Jacques Delors's salary.

Correction. It turns out that not all fish are cod after all. I have discovered three further kinds of Euro-fish. There are "cohesion fish", which apparently are those given by rich countries to poor ones. Then there are "foreign fish". Foreign fish swim in Canadian or Russian water. And finally there are "paper fish". Paper fish don't actually exist, but *they might do one day* when stocks are replenished.

I can't believe it. I've just discovered whole shoals more. There are "Accelerated Cohesion Fish", and "Other people's fish", and the Irish horse mackerel or "skag", which migrates to Norway: the Irish say that although the fish have swum away from Ireland they are still Irish but the Norwegians say that... well, you can imagine how the argument goes.

On the radio this morning someone was saying that in Europe *snails* are fish (land-based). Can someone tell me how it is possible to know whether or not this is a joke?

It isn't.

April 19

My Euro-file is bulging. I had intended to take a number of items for your instruction and/or entertainment, and put them into some adroitly-crafted order which would give this article a coherent shape and possibly even a narrative flow. This has proved impossible, partly because of lack of time caused by a day which went missing at the weekend for reasons which are none of your concern, and partly because the nature of this material is inherently not conducive to coherence. That sentence shows that I have been reading more Euro-prose than is good for me.

So, diving into the file at random I find a press release which comes from Stan Newens, Member of the European Parliament (London Central). It starts as follows: "There is no doubt that one of the prime needs today in a multicultural world is that people should be able to understand one another."

How true. How very, very true. It is, as the poet Alexander Pope put it, "What oft was thought but ne'er so well expressed." What a pity that in the next sentence Mr Newens blows it completely: "It is very desirable we should encourage the learning of foreign languages to a much greater extent but in my experience only a limited number of people can learn any number and then not very thoroughly."

Evidently Mr Newens has not mastered the English language very thoroughly. Perhaps this is why he is so keen on Esperanto. "However controlled experiments have shown that Esperanto, taught as an apprentice language will reduce the learning time of a foreign language and provide the use of Esperanto as a living language." Perhaps that sentence sounds better in Esperanto. Or perhaps it *is* in Esperanto.

I felt I should know more about Stan Newens and turned to the invaluable *The New Europe,* edited by Victor Keegan and Martin Kettle. Here I find that Stanley Newens (Labour Co-op) was born in 1930, went to University College London, and has been a miner and a teacher. He has five children and he is married. His languages are given as German, French, Spanish, Dutch and Polish. No mention of Esperanto. Or, come to think of it, English.

Be that as it may, in the last Euro-election the polyglot Mr Newens was elected with 78,561 votes out of 186,340 cast in a constituency with an electorate of 493,019. So he got in with fewer than half the votes cast, and a huge majority of the electorate didn't vote at all. Using only one side of the paper discuss in not more than 100 words what this tells us about 1. The First Past The Post System. 2. The desirability of Proportional Representation. 3. The level of interest in Europe (lack of) shown by the people of Central London.

The Conservative in that election got 67,019, and the Green got a creditable 28,087. The Also Rans included Lord Sutch (Official Monster Raving Loony, 841) and Lindy St-Claire (Corrective Party, 707). Sad to relate, the Humanist candidate got only 304.

Lindy St-Claire also stood in the recent Newbury by-election, and naturally got my vote. I don't know whether she is planning to stand in the area in the Euro-elections. If so perhaps I could form an alliance between the Raving Loony party, the Corrective Party and the Boston Tea Party. On second thoughts this is not a good idea. This is a matter that has to be taken seriously if I am to get elected and lay my hands on the huge salary and mega-perks.

While on the subject of alliances, I have received a letter from Keith Flett, the celebrated writer of letters. He is suggesting a merger between my party and the Save Steve Platt For Socialism Campaign. Steve Platt is (was?) editor of the *New Statesman* and is at the centre of a row of considerable complexity.

Since I try to avoid writing letters I phoned Mr Flett who explained that it was all about beards. Duncan Campbell (not the *Guardian's* Duncan Campbell but the other one) who is (was?) Chairman of the *New Statesman* is clean-shaven. Steve Platt has a beard. I asked Mr Flett if *he* has a beard. "Of course," he said, rather crossly.

I have no wish to become involved in the internal wranglings of the *New Statesman* and this business about beards strikes me as frivolous. At least it did until I had another look at Keegan and Kettle's Euro-tome. The thumb-nail sketches of the 81 UK Members of the European Parliament are accompanied by mug-shots. Analysis of these shows twelve of them to be identifiably female. Of the men, four are Lords, four are Sirs, two are Revs and one is an Hon.

What is even more interesting is that out of the 69 male MEPs no fewer than nine wear a moustache, and eight have a moustache and beard. So almost exactly a quarter of the UK MEPs (male) are not clean-shaven. This must be as unrepresentative of the electorate as a whole as is the proportion of male to female MEPs.

If we break down these findings on party lines we find the following results for UK MEPs (male). Conservative moustaches, two. Conservative moustache and beards, three. Moustache (Labour) five. Moustache and beard (Labour) six.

Which reminds me that the Vice-President of the Regional Council of Guadeloupe was had up last week in a fraud case (see *Libération* April 14) involving 50 units of public housing of which only 25 were actually built. His name is José Moustache.

Meanwhile back in Strasbourg only three UK Conservative MEPs wear glasses, as against 16 Labour (this includes women). I have as yet no information on the subject of MEP contact lenses.

I can only find two MEPs with the full set — moustache, beard and glasses. One is David Bowe, (Cleveland and Yorkshire North), Labour, born 1955, Sunderland Poly, Bath University and Teesside Poly. Job: Teacher. The other is Llewellyn Smith (South East Wales, Labour). Born 1944. Cardiff University. Job: Tutor-organiser.

April 28

Last week I had a phone call from the Returning Officer. Let's call him Mr Smith. As it happens, that is his name. He wanted to talk about my nomination paper. Faithful readers may remember that I recently described the nomination paper, where there are boxes in which I have to give my address, full name and "Description". I said I had finally decided to go along with the girl from Ipanema and describe myself as "Tall and tanned and young and lovely."

Mr Smith was ringing to say that he had seen the article and that he felt he should warn me that he will not be able to accept that description. Why? I asked. Did he think it was inaccurate? No, he said, it's just that you're only allowed six words.

My first thought was simply to take out one of the ands, but that spoils the rhythm. I'll have to think of something else. Campaign for Real Life? No Taxation Without Representation Party? Give Me The Job And Money Party? I can't go on dithering like this. We politicians must be firm and decisive, and time is running out. I think I'll stick with The Boston Tea Party.

Mr Smith's other news is that he can at last confirm that we in the Newbury District of Berkshire (now that at this late hour the French have finally signed something or other) are no longer in Wiltshire but definitely in North Hampshire and Oxford.

I should explain, for reasons that will soon become clear, that this telephone conversation was accompanied by the sound of hammering. This came from Mr Gargery, who is mending a hole where the rain comes in. In this case Gargery isn't his real name, but that's what I call him because he reminds me of Bernard Miles in the film of *Great Expectations*. He talks like Joe Gargery, and looks like Joe Gargery, and he always has a hammer in his hand. Whatever job he undertakes it seems to involve hammer and nails. I suspect he saws wood with a hammer. As well as always having a hammer in his hand he usually has nails of assorted sizes gripped in his mouth, as is the manner of cobblers.

Joe has a big transit van. The side of it used to be like a huge nomination paper. It had his name, address and description — Builder and Decorator. Recently he split up with Mrs Gargery and is keeping a low profile. At nighttime his van is parked outside the house of a lady who is not Mrs Gargery. To minimise gossip he has painted out the words on the side of the vehicle, which is now known locally as Clint — The Van With No Name.

With Joe Gargery hammering overhead (though as far as my concentration goes it might as well have been on my head) I tried to assess the current state of the party. In a morale-raising speech to myself I pointed out that it is a mathematical certainty that I will win this election. Look at it this way. The constituency is about 550,000 electors. In Belgium the turn-out in Euro-elections is about 90 per cent, in Luxembourg 88 per cent, and in Italy 80 per cent. The UK is far the lowest at about 35 per cent. So we're looking at a probable turn-out of, let's say, about 185,000.

Say there are four serious candidates — the three main parties and me. In that case there probably won't be anyone with an absolute majority, but that's the way the First Past The Post system works. I should be safely in if I get 50,000 but let's make sure and go for a ton.

Now for the mathematics. I started my campaign 16 weeks before the election with only two supporters. In the first week I gained four more and in the second I won over eight. You will see that new supporters were coming in at a rate of double each week. If I continue like this (and why not?) in the last week of the campaign I will get 80,000 new voters, and that's in addition to the 80,000 or so accumulated in the previous fifteen weeks. Home and dry.

The hammering stopped for a moment and I heard a voice from on high say something between clenched nails. It was hard to make out, but it sounded like "Wishful thinking. Impossible."

Impossible is a word that keeps coming to mind. If not quite impossible it is extremely difficult for an individual to find out how to go about this whole business. There is no "Guide to Candidates" for the Europarliament, as I gather there is for Westminster (though I haven't managed to track one down). Brian Smith, the Returning Officer, has been extremely helpful but sometimes when I ask a question he has to refer to circulars he has received from the Home Office.

I don't want to trouble him all the time so I asked the Home Office if they issue these circulars to prospective candidates. Not normally, came the reply. I was about to embark on a discussion of what was the Home Office's definition of normality but decided that life, time and my temper were too short. It's very important to stay calm, and the doctor has said no more than three beta-blockers a day and go easy on the Ribena.

It's difficult, though. I sometimes feel I'm playing a game without being able to see the rule book. Sometimes I feel that I'm not even playing the game: I'm the ball.

Dealing with these Euro-matters I have come up against two kinds of people. There are those who find the whole thing a bit of a farce and a giggle. And there are those who are in deadly earnest and consider the whole thing to be no laughing matter, either in general or detail, whether they're for or against. This second lot are like cats: they *hate* being laughed at.

Not, of course, that I am referring to Mrs Josephine Meek at the Home Office. She was the one who said the circulars were not issued normally. She referred me to *Schofield's Election Law*, published by Shaw and Sons in two very large volumes. I would find it in any large library, she said. But I don't live anywhere near a large library. There's a mobile library that visits the village for quarter of an hour once a fortnight and very good it is too, but I doubt if it has *Schofield's Election Law* in two very large volumes. Or the Representation of the People Act 1983, or the European Parliamentary Election Act 1986, cmnd 2209, or Schedule 1, for 1983. Large library means Reading or Oxford. I don't drive. Taxis, trains, time and money. Why should it be so hard to find out how to exercise my democratic rights?

"I need an Agent," I groaned out loud. I really do, there's so much to be done.

"I'll be your Agent," Gargery said from the roof. I didn't know I had been thinking out loud. "I won't vote for you," he said. "I'm going to vote for Jo Hawkins (Lib Dem) but I don't mind being your Agent. Drive you around and that."

Archimedes and the bath, Bruce and the spider, Newton and the apple, Watt and the kettle. It was one of those moments. Clint, the Van With No Name, would be the ideal campaign bus.

I couldn't quite make out what Gargery said as he drove off, hammer in hand, but it sounded like "What larks, Pip old chap, what larks."

May 3

In South Africa the first free elections are being held. Those pictures of seemingly endless queues patiently waiting to cast their votes were immensely moving. They also served to remind me that the Euro-elections are upon us and that in only a few weeks' time we will be witnessing just such scenes here in the constituency of North Hampshire and Oxford. The market squares outside the Town Halls, and the country lanes leading to the local schools and Village Halls, will be blocked solid with simple Berkshire folk eagerly waiting for their turn at the ballot boxes and their chance to cast their votes for the Boston Tea Party and thus to turn the tide of history.

Cometh the hour, cometh the man. We must go forward unflinchingly on the path to which destiny has called us, without fear or favour, without false hopes or hoarse throats. I can already hear the rolling phrases. This brave venture... We must learn to look forward into the past, not back into the future... Nor shall my sword sleep in my hand... As Returning Officer of the Constituency it is my duty to inform you that the aforesaid Boston, Richard (hushed voice, "Tea Party") has therefore been duly elected to serve...

But that's all six weeks away and there's many a slip 'twixt cup and counting your chickens. I have completed my nomination papers, with the required 30 signatures with their numbers on the electoral roll. What is now of immediate interest is my leaflets, which I have to get written, designed, and printed in plenty of time for the Royal Mail to deliver them in time. I am entitled to one free delivery to each elector. That means copying onto envelopes the names and addresses of more than half a million people. Joe Gargery, my Agent, is a hard-working chap but I just can't see him getting through it, not even if I give him a hand.

Fortunately the Royal Mail offers an alternative deal. They will take unaddressed leaflets, not even in an envelope, and put one through each letter-box in the constituency. Actually they don't call them letter-boxes but delivery points. Thus a hotel or hospital, for example, will get just one leaflet, as will each "house with one main front door". This will bring the number down to something over 200,000, which still looks like being a hefty printing bill, and after Mr Boston's fall at the thirteenth in the Grand National the coffers are desperately empty.

What actually happens to all these election leaflets? They come through the letter-box and for days litter the entrance along with the other junk mail. Finally you scoop them up and put them in the waste-paper basket. They then stay there till rubbish collection day when you put the whole lot in the wheely-bin. This is where the Boston Tea Party is different from any other. We will go from house to house and put the leaflets *straight in the wheely-bin*. It'll save your time and it won't litter your hall. You know it makes sense.

Gargery has come up with another scheme. We could show that we're really, really environment-friendly by not printing any leaflets at all.

Meanwhile I am preparing my bridgehead into Europe ("bridgehead: an area of ground secured or to be taken on the enemy's side of an obstacle."). Wining and dining will be one of my main occupations as an MEP. This is confirmed by Roy Jenkins's *European Diary 1977-1981*, which should not be confused with his memoirs, *A Life at the Centre*. The latter are hardly in the Alan Clark league as entertainment, but they are a hoot compared with the *European Diary* which is a real crasher. One reason for treating the Common Market with deep suspicion is that it has produced such stunningly boring books, the latest example being Leon Brittan's *Europe: the Europe we need* (Hamish Hamilton £17.99). My vague memory of Leon Brittan at Cambridge more than 30 years ago was that he was boring even then. Now he bores for Europe.

Roy Jenkins's tome is less a diary in the Pepys sense than in that of the diary on your desk in which your various secretaries write down your appointments. A typical entry will tell you little more than what the weather was like and who Jenks had lunch with. The index provides a useful short cut. For example: "Baudouin, King of the Belgians... lunch with

RJ,142,180... RJ entertains to dinner, 291-2." "Tugendhat, Christopher... qualities, 33; dines with RJ, 35, 206, 129n, ...as sole supporter of RJ,546,603; meets Queen Elizabeth, 648; assassination attempt on, 651-2." Then there is the entry on the Committee of Permanent Representatives (COREPER) who are evidently a hungry lot. It includes "dinners for,122; lunches, 141, 187, 212, 219, 264, 272, 321, 354, 486, 519-20, 523, 533, 563, 583, 617, 653"

The best entry is "Vredeling, Henk... lunch with RJ, 462: breaks glass, 505". I don't claim to have read the whole of the book but I would be surprised if this is not its high point:

> Tuesday 25 September 1979. The main interest of the dinner emerged only in retrospect. Vredeling, the fourth member of the Commission present, was next to me and appeared throughout to be perfectly sober. However, at some stage after 12.15 a.m. he got involved in an affair with 'Chrystal'. I was not sure, when it was first reported to me, whether this was a form of glass or a German lady. It subsequently became clear that it was a question of glass, for in a fit of anger with some Dutch MEP at some unspecified time later in the night, he had picked up a heavy ashtray, thrown it, missed (I suppose fortunately) the MEP, lightly grazed the chandelier and shattered a plate glass window. The cost was £5,000; the cost to Vredeling's morale was much higher.

What larks, Pip old chap, what larks!

May 17

The Rubicon has been crossed. The die has been cast. On Monday Gargery and I got in The Van With No Name, drove to Abingdon with the necessary papers, and handed over the lolly provided by the *Guardian* for the deposit. A couple of days later Postman Fat brings me a letter the gist of which is that "I HEREBY GIVE YOU NOTICE that I have decided that the nomination paper received by me, nominating you as a candidate for the Hampshire North and Oxford constituency, and signed by N. Williams as proposer and Heather Macaulay as Seconder, is a valid nomination. (Signed) B.M. Smith. Acting Returning Officer."

This was soon followed by a poster entitled NOTICE OF POLL. This shows that I am clearly going to win because alphabetical order has put my name at the top of the list. There are seven candidates, giving their "Description (if any)" as respectively the Boston Tea Party, Natural Law Party, Liberal Democrat, Official Conservative, Labour, UK Independence and Green Party.

The most intriguing name on the list (apart, of course, from my own) is that of David George John Wilkinson, standing for the UK Independence Party. His proposer is Dacre of Glanton (a.k.a. Hugh Trevor-Roper) and the seconder is Norman Stone. Professor Stone's views about the European elections are, er, erratic. He said on the box the other day that voting in the European elections is like being invited to go shopping for vegetables in a still life. What *can* this mean?

Which brings us effortlessly back to the subject of the European Community and food. I am still plodding through Roy Jenkins's *European Diary 1977-1981*. I have already quoted from this massive and massively boring tome the incident in which late at night a European Commisioner in his cups caused some £5,000 of damage by hurling a weighty crystal ashtray. At that time I thought it was the only passage of interest in the whole book but my diligence has been rewarded by finding a few others.

For example Jenks tells us that on 13 March 1979 "Just before the end of the Council, Callaghan and I both went out and coincided in the loo, whereupon he made me the most fanciful offer, saying, 'Would you like to be Governor of Hong Kong?'"

Why don't I have fanciful offers like that with Prime Ministers I coincide with in the loo?

During his European years Roy seems to have consumed an awesome quantity of lunches and dinners. Such is his enthusiasm for the pleasures of the table that when at one point he refers to an associate of Tony Benn's as "a pudding of a woman" I thought for a terrible moment that he would pour cream over her, sprinkle on some sugar and scoff her.

But even Jenks was impressed when he found himself sitting at dinner next to Liam Cosgrave, the Irish Foreign Minister. Cosgrave, says Roy, "distinguished himself by eating more than any man I have ever seen." The main course was roast beef. Jenkins hesitates between taking one or two pieces, and takes one. He does not take a second helping. By contrast the mightily carnivorous Cosgrave "took four for a first helping and three for a second helping, and followed this by two enormous helpings of ice-cream *gâteau*."

Mr Cosgrave then slept for most of the rest of the evening, having evidently made a massive contribution to reducing the European Food Mountain. Jenks meanwhile was adding to the Word Mountain. Take this, for example, but take a deep breath first. On 2 August 1977 Roy "did a general summing-up, of which the main import was that as the harsh reality was that none of the three main governments, France, Germany or Britain, was prepared to support a major Commission initiative, we, combined with trying to get certain urgent, practical things through, had to be prepared to go against them and to blaze a trail to a greater extent than we had done previously, however much this offended people, and that the obvious direction for this was monetary union."

This raises quite a few issues, and it is only reasonable that my constituents should be left in no doubt as to my stance thereupon. I am in favour of monetary union.

Every time I go abroad I have to change my money from that of the country whence I am going to that whither I goeth. This makes a fat profit for banks and money-changers, and a fat loss for me. I would like to be able to use the same currency in Athens as in Aberdeen, in Manchester as Madrid. And that's an end on't.

The other point raised by the long Jenkins quote is its astounding arrogance. The commission, as personified by Roy, knows best and thinks nothing of going against the wishes of the Governments of France, Germany and Britain, "however much this offended people." That is to say the people who elect governments. It is tedious to spell this out, but these governments, however dreadful they may be, were elected. Roy and his merry men (almost without exception they are men) were not elected. They were appointed. The rest of us were disappointed.

As I follow the campaign trail (head held high, charisma dazzling, mental and physical agility that of a man twice my age) I often find myself comparing the workings of the European Community with my only previous venture into politics. This was on the Parish Council. There were no parties (in the political sense), the electorate was only about 150, we raised our own taxes (it's called a precept and for the whole village is currently about £ 900 a year), nobody was paid, nobody ever claimed expenses, and we got things done. We replanted trees after the devastation of Dutch Elm Disease and the two hurricanes. With jumble sales and raffles and collections we raised enough to extend the village hall so it could double as a cricket pavilion. Without knowing it we were, I suppose, putting into practice the principle of what in Brussels and Maastricht is called subsidiarity; that is to say, we were performing tasks which can be most effectively carried out at an immediate or local level.

And this is something which is hated in Brussels and in Westminster and in Whitehall, and which is why the Thatcherite and neo-Thatcherite governments have smashed local government.

Now I must get down to important matters like getting Boston T-shirts made, and Boston Tea-bags, and Boston Tea-towels and Boston Tea-pots. So much to do, so little time.

May 26

Excitement at Boston Tea Party HQ with the arrival of the first badges and Boston T-shirts. These are only samples, but if all goes well we should have ample supplies quite soon. Possibly (no promises, mind you) before the election.

There also arrived copies of my election address (or communication). This document is in clear contravention of the law since it doesn't bear the name and address either of the printer or publisher, which is in flagrant thingummy of the Representation of the People's Act, not to mention Magna Carta and the Ten Commandments. Unfortunately the enthusiasm of my supporters is such that they simply disregarded the legal niceties and in spite of my best endeavours headed off to distribute the leaflets in various licensed premises in the vicinity. What could I do, M'Lud? I throw myself upon the mercy of the court.

ELECTION COMMUNICATION

Election of Member of the European Parliament for the constituency of North Hampshire and Oxford.
RICHARD BOSTON — BOSTON TEA PARTY

An MEP (Member of the European Parliament) gets £31,678 a year.

Not bad, but that's just the start of it.

Subsistence allowance of 190 ECU (about £155) per day for attending meetings in the European Community, plus cost of accommodation and meals.

A general expenditure allowance of £2,131 per month for office management costs. This is halved in respect of members who "for no valid reason" have failed to attend at least half the number of plenary sessions. (So the poor Italian MEP who hasn't been to Strasbourg for *three years* has been getting hardly more than £12,000 a year for office expenses and for doing nothing.)

Travel rate allowance of 57p per kilometre (about twice what the AA reckons it costs to run a car) for the first 800 kilometres, 29p for each additional kilometre within the Community to attend meetings. Plus £2,340 per annum for travel on official business other than to attend official meetings (also known as "jaunts" or "hols").

£5,826 a month for "Secretarial Assistance Allowance" — that's nearly £70,000 a year to spend on "secretaries".

And so on.

That's the trough
I want to get my snout in it
I WANT THE JOB
I WANT THE MONEY
I WANT THE PERKS
I WANT YOUR VOTE

Richard Boston has lived in the Newbury District of the Euro-constituency of North Hampshire and Oxford for more than 20 years, and has served as Chairman of Aldworth Parish Council (unpaid). He founded and edited the environmental magazine the *Vole* which went bust. He has written for the *Guardian* for donkey's years, and is the author of several books.

The next day I went to Oxford where, as usual, it was raining. Oxford is not far away, and the Ashmolean is my favourite museum, so for the last 20 years or so I've been to Oxford four or five times a year. I can only remember one occasion when the sun was shining, and I can only remember one occasion when it wasn't raining. Oxford rain is a drizzling wretched sort of rain that feels like distilled pessimism mixed with misery. If Cambridge is the coldest place on earth (which it is), Oxford is the wettest.

So it was not surprising that I got drenched in the ten-minute walk from the station to what Jay Gatsby would have called Oggsford College. Indeed it was the Oxford College of Further Education which, with something like 12,000 students, must be as big as the University. Unfortunately it was raining too hard to check on such details.

The College was holding a Europe Week. Gareth Morris of the Languages and Humanities Dept. had invited all seven local candidates for the European Parliament to spend the morning in Lecture Theatre D to say a few words and answer a few questions, or make complete fools of themselves, as they preferred.

The candidates were standing for (in alphabetical order): the Boston Tea Party, Conservative, Green, Labour, Lib Dem, Natural Law, and UK Independent. We were all on parade at 9.30 in the morning which was not bad considering the distances some of us had to travel. All of us, that is, except for the Conservative candidate who, like Macavity, was not there.

He had been invited, quite some time ago, but already had a prior engagement. He had then been invited to field a substitute but this too was declined. He can't be blamed really. A self-declared Tory round here is in risk of being torn limb from limb. Not literally, but you know what I mean. The Conservatives got a terrible drubbing in the Newbury by-election, and in the recent local elections didn't win a single seat in Oxford. This bit of Berkshire and the Vale of the White Horse and Oxford was rock-solid Conservative until only a few years ago. It would not be true to say that Conservatives are now unpopular: they are actively disliked. I'm not surprised Mr Mather didn't turn up or even field a substitute.

That's his name. Graham Christopher Spencer Mather. Solicitor. President of the European Policy Forum. Born 23 October 1954. Son of Thomas and Doreen Mather. Hutton Grammar school. Member of Westminster City Council 1982-86.

In his absence we discussed how his name was pronounced. Some said the first syllable would be as in the merry month of May. Others rhymed the name with father. But somebody who seemed to know led us to gather that Mather rhymes with gather (which meant that we could go (all together now) "Oh dear, where can the Mather be?" Which we did.

There was an audience of well over a hundred, faced by a panel consisting of me plus the following: The Chairman, Chairperson or Chair. The Invisible Man (Graham Mather, Cons). The Labour Candidate, John Tanner. This was indeed a surprise because John Tanner is a character in *Man And Superman*. Shaw's stage direction describes John Tanner as follows: "He is too young to be described simply as a big man with a beard. But it is already plain that middle life will find him in that category. He has still some of the slimness of youth, but youthfulness is not the effect he aims at... He is prodigiously fluent of speech, restless, excitable (mark the snorting nostril and the restless blue eye, just the thirty-secondth of an inch too wide open), possibly a little mad."

The John Tanner of today has a moustache but no beard and he displays no obvious signs of being even a little mad. Otherwise he doesn't seem to have changed much since Shaw wrote his play nearly a century ago.

Then there was the Lib Dem, Jo Hawkins. She's the one I have to fear. She is widely tipped to win. (Incidentally, I have tried and failed to get a bookmaker to give odds on this race. Can anyone help?) Clearly she won't come in first because I'm going to, but she could come in a very close second. We have a pact, which I would never have revealed in public if she hadn't. It concerns the vast secretarial expenses claimable by an MEP. When I am elected she will be my secretary. In the unlikely event of her being elected, I will be her secretary.

Then there was the Green, Mike Woodin. I don't think I have to take him very seriously. As founder and editor of the *Vole* my environmentalist credentials are such that I can pull rank on any such come-latelies.

Next comes Hugh Godfrey of the Natural Law Party. He was born in Kent in 1938. So was I. He has run a number of Pizza restaurants. I have eaten in a number of Pizza restaurants. Remarkable coincidences. The Natural Law Party is the political wing of the Maharishi's Transcendental Meditation outfit. He talked about Yogic Flying, but instead of doing something impressive like levitating he banged on about how groups of people all Yogic Flying at once brought down the crime rate and stopped wars and he made all sorts of other claims which were hard not to laugh at. Impossible not to laugh at.

Actually I owe him an apology because a couple of days later he sent me a quantity of literature containing scientific papers backing up points I had challenged. Somewhere at the back of my mind I had slotted this lot in with the likes of the Moonies and the Scientologists (who give me the creeps). This was wrong. I still have reservations about the Natural Law Party, but I would congratulate Hugh Godfrey on his politeness, correctness and calmness in the face of derision, and as soon as I am elected and have plenty of leisure will look seriously into Yogic Flying which is, I'm sure, the only way to travel.

Finally there was the UK Independence candidate David Wilkinson, who is resolutely against the Common Market, EEC, EU or whatever it is called. He told me he had attended a "Counter-Summit" in Strasbourg last October, having cycled all the way from Arras, which is a tremendous distance, especially as he had no money or food. Naturally he was very hungry indeed when he arrived and could not refuse the invitation from a Danish MEP to lunch at a very posh restaurant by the Cathedral along with 200 (yes, two hundred) other guests. Could this be the Strasbourg restaurant which has just received its third Michelin star?

The meeting went pleasantly enough and the next day I rang up Graham Mather. I didn't mention Banquo's ghost but I said that he had been conspicuous by his absence at the Oxford meeting. He said that he had had a prior meeting, canvassing somewhere else. The conversation then went along these lines.

Boston: Where?
Mather: I don't want to tell you. Are you you asking me as a fellow candidate or as a writer for the *Guardian?*
Boston: Writing for the *Guardian.*
Mather: Don't you find a conflict of interest in being a candidate and reporting on it?
Boston: No
Mather: Have you looked into the legal aspect of what you are doing?
Boston: No
(Brief pause)
Boston: If you have no further questions perhaps I could ask you some.
Mather: I think I've said enough, old boy. All the best. Bye.
   And he put the phone down.

May 31

The size of a Euro-constituency is absurd. My electorate is well over half a million and I've only met a tiny fraction of them in spite of non-stop canvassing. Both in the pub and in the village shop. I've got speaking engagements in Oxford, Newbury and Harwell. People keep telling me I ought to be kissing babies. I can't see the point. They don't have a vote.

During the summer every Sunday and Bank Holiday there is a bus service along the whole of the Ridgeway from Reading to Swindon, four buses a day. It's called the Ridgeway Explorer and £4.75 gives an adult unlimited travel on this route and all other bus services in Wiltshire for the day. (Children and OAPs £3.50. Families (up to two adults and two children) £9.50.)

I still haven't worked out the precise boundaries of my constituency-to-be but this bus route must pass through quite a bit of it. On Sunday the bus was hijacked for my campaign, a scheme which was masterminded by Bryan McAllister who had turned up with a bunch of chums.

First I posed for photographs with Peter Jay, the former Ambassador to the United States, and more recently employee of the late Robert Maxwell and something important in television. He has no connection with my campaign. He was just captaining the visiting team in the village cricket match. We were just chatting, and someone decided that this was what he called a photo-opportunity. That's all.

We all got on the bus (except for Peter Jay) and I found myself chatting in a free-wheeling sort of manner to an agreeable Australian gentleman. After about twenty minutes I saw out of the corner of my eye what looked like a microphone. It was a microphone. And there was a camera too. In fact there was a crew of five from the Australian Broadcasting Corporation. If you happen to be in Australia on June 14 watch "Foreign Correspondent" at 9.30pm, and there I'll be. What surprises me is that Australian television has picked up on my candidature (candidacy?) while the *Newbury Weekly News* still hasn't.

The good news is that we've got masses of badges now. An insomniac called Robert turned up with badges and Boston Tea-shirts, one of which he flogged to Australian television, which I thought was rather clever. Then we stopped for cream teas at Britchcombe Farm near Uffington, where we were joined by Shaw Taylor, who McAllister had roped in as my advisor on personal security which it is generally agreed is something all politicians need.

The route goes through leafy lanes past tiny villages. The population density all the way is extremely low so I won't have picked up many (or any) votes. Never mind, a good time was had by all, and the outing made me realise that this must be a contender for Most Beautiful Constituency In Europe. But, as I started off by saying, it is enormous. It is made up of six Westminster parliamentary constituencies. Or is it seven? As a candidate I now have the right to have a copy of the electoral register. Fortunately I asked for the lists in only two parliamentary constituencies, in spite of which the pile of paper I have received is 14 inches high and weighs nearly two stone. Six days a week the postman staggers to my door, out of breath, heart pounding, red in the face, grunting and groaning under the weight of electoral lists. I commiserated with him on Saturday and he confirmed that a postman's lot is not a happy one. Not that he minded lugging all these parcels about. No, it's the dogs. He said that in his 20 years as a postman he has had a total of 105 stitches for dog bites and he said there were others in the local sorting office who have had more.

Since there are no votes to be got out of saying anything about dogs other than how wonderful they are I will switch tack and get back to the matter in hand which, most pressingly, is writing my speech for tomorrow.

Now, (I shall say, sipping from a glass containing a colourless liquid), as I go up and down the country, talking to people in all walks of life (including, if I may bring in a personal note, myself) I am often asked a question which is deceptively simple. Why, they ask, is it called the Boston Tea Party?

Why (was my initial reply) not? But somehow this seemed too frivolous a reply, not to say facetious. Facetious is a very interesting word. It contains all the vowels, and in their correct order, and is shorter than its rival which is abstemious.

Where was I? Yes, the Boston Tea Party. I turned to the *Encyclopedia Britannica*, eleventh edition, 1911, where all is made instantly clear. The Tea Act of 1773 was defied by emptying three cargoes of tea into Boston harbour on 16 December 1773. This was done by citizens disguised as Red Indians. Great Britain replied with "various penal regulations and recontructive acts of government." Finally the port of Boston was closed, with results that move the *Britannica* out of prose and into poetry.

> Not even a ferry, a scow or other boat could move in the harbour. Marblehead and Salem were made ports of entry, and Salem was made the capital. But they would not profit by Boston's misfortune. The people covenanted not to use British goods and to suspend trade with Great Britain... Finally came war, with Lexington and Bunker Hill, and beleaguerment by the colonial army; until on the 17th of March the British were compelled by Washington to evacuate the city. With them went about 1,100 Tory refugees, many of them of the finest families of the city and province. The evacuation closed the heroic period of Boston's history. War did not again approach the city.

These are indeed stirring words (what's a scow?) and they are clearly relevant to our present situation. Like the people of Boston more than two centuries ago, we today resent taxation without representation. We dislike being ruled at a distance. And when I speak of a distance (my image consultant says that at this point I should not overdo the Arthur Scargill stabbing gesture with the right index finger), I repeat that when I speak of being ruled from a distance I do not just mean Brussels or Strasbourg. I also mean Westminster and Whitehall.

And now I want to talk about my friend Satish Kumar for reasons which will soon become apparent. Nowadays Satish edits the excellent magazine *Resurgence* but I first met him some 30 years ago when he was on a walk. A long walk. A very long walk. He was born in Northern India and became a Jain mendicant monk. Jains are vegetarian and adhere strictly to the principle of *ahimsa* which means avoiding harm to any living being. They walk slowly so as to avoid harming insects or plants, and even sweep the ground in front of them for the same reason.

After eight years as a monk Satish went to the ashram of Gandhi's disciple Vinoba Bhave. Then he heard that Bertrand Russell had been arrested for civil disobedience in protest against nuclear weapons. And he thought that if a man of 90 can take a stand like that then a young man like him should do something too. So with his friend Prabhakar Menon he undertook a Peace March to the capital cities of the nuclear powers. They walked from India to Moscow, to Paris, to London, to Washington.

They took no weapons for self-defence. They took no money. They ate no meat. They set out in 1962 from Gandhi's grave, and they were given lavish hospitality in Teheran and in Moscow; they were arrested in Paris, met Bertrand Russell in England and Martin Luther King in the USA. They walked 8,000 miles from the grave of the assassinated Gandhi to that of the assassinated J.F. Kennedy.

I hope this has a general relevance to the Boston Tea Party. The specific relevance is in a small incident in Russia. When they were visiting a tea factory a woman gave them four packets of tea. She asked them to deliver one packet each to Khruschev, de Gaulle, Macmillan and Kennedy. And they should tell them all that if they ever thought of pressing the button to start dropping nuclear bombs, they should have a cup of tea instead.

That's what I call a real tea party.

June 7

It's amazing to think that this time next week I will be a Member of the European Parliament. I will be wealthy beyond the dreams of avarice, with a fat salary, enormous expenses, perks of every kind, and the MEP's favourite restaurant in Strasbourg with three Michelin stars. Let the good times roll.

This election is a horse race all the way. To start with it's a first-past-the-post contest. I can't say that voting systems have ever been near the top of my list of things to think about but as the campaign has continued I have very much come round to being in favour of a single transferable vote. Or some such system which would make it more like an each-way bet. What I mean is that (in the unlikely event of my not being elected) I know who I would like to be. Unfortunately under the present system you can't vote twice unless you're a bird, as Sir Boyle Roche (1743-1807) is said to have said. Also attributed to him is "Mr Speaker, I smell a rat; I see him forming in the air and darkening the sky; but I'll nip him in the bud."

A few days ago, when we candidates were still, as it were, under starter's orders, I wouldn't (frankly) have given myself good odds. Then I came a cropper by investing my campaign funds on Mister Boston in the Grand National.

I had a similar setback last week when I came down with what was either Dutch Elm Disease or the worst hay fever I have ever suffered. This meant that I was unable to go to a number of public meetings at which I had planned to perform feats of oratory that would have linked my name for all time with those of Cicero and Demosthenes.

There seem to be a number of people round here who have been hit by this ailment. Many of them have never had hay fever before. Opinion in the pub blames it on oilseed rape, which is (of course) the fault of the European agricultural policy.

This enforced respite in the campaign turns out to be the best thing that could have happened because you can't come up from behind if you're in front. It has always been part of my strategy not to peak too soon. The correctness of this policy was exemplified in the Derby last week. Erhaab was nearly last at the top of Tattenham Hill. Two furlongs out he was ten lengths off the leader and then (in the words of Chris Hawkins in the *Guardian*) "the colt found a stunning turn of foot... to win in the end with a touch of nonchalance by a length and a quarter". It really was extraordinary to watch. It seemed as though the nag had suddenly found an extra gear, was turbo-driven, jet-propelled or something. It overtook the other horses like a Lamborghini passing a postman on a bicycle.

Chris Hawkins described Mister Boston as a good stayer with some form on the soft. It is that staying power (and form on the soft) that I must show in these final days running up to the election. Then, like Erhaab, I will surge ahead with (in Chris Hawkins's nicely turned phrase) a touch of nonchalance.

The rest of the EC votes on Sunday. We don't, because it was written in Magna Carta that Britons ever more shall vote on Thursdays. This means that we'll be voting on Thursday but can't start counting the votes until Sunday in case our outcome should influence the choice of the people across the Channel. The upshot is that between Thursday and Sunday there is a hiatus.

And so, fellow citizens, I give this message to you as you go to the polls on Thursday. Vote early, and vote often.

June 14

Mather 72,809
Hawkins 63,015
Wilkinson 8,377
Woodin 7,311
Tanner 4,852

Godfrey 1,027
Boston 1,018

Reeling from its shock defeat at the polls on Sunday night the BTP (Boston Tea Party) went into an emergency session in the early hours of Monday morning. White-faced members of the party's executive were tight-lipped in their refusal to speculate openly about the party's future.

Even so, there is general agreement that the Boston Tea Party's image requires modernisation. It may possibly even need refurbishment. This is the only way in which this great party to which we belong can capture the apathy constituency, which is huge. (Scarcely more than a third of the electorate turned out for this Euro-election.)

The Candidate has responded to his critics in a manner which has been described by some observers as volatile. His first comment on not being elected was, "Well, you won't have Richard Milhous Boston to kick around any more." This remark has been considered in poor taste since it clearly refers to the late Richard Nixon who is scarcely cold in his grave (or crematorium, as the case may be) and ex-President Nixon was a liar and acclaimed by all leading politicians and is therefore a role model who should only be spoken about in terms of reverence.

On not being elected the Candidate started singing from Handel's Messiah. The bit about "He was rejected." Not satisfied with this he quoted the full text of the 53rd chapter of the Book of Isaiah, the 53rd chapter, which begins:

1. Who hath believed our report? and to whom is the arm of the Lord revealed?
2. For he shall grow up before him as a tender plant, and as a root out of a dry ground: he hath no form nor comeliness; and when we shall see him, there is no beauty that we should desire him.
3. He is despised and rejected of men; a man of sorrows, and acquainted with grief.

In Handel's version it then goes on to a strange bit in which he says "He gave his back to the smiters, and his cheeks to them that plucked off the hair, and his cheeks to them that plucked off the hair. He hid not his face from shame and spitting, He hid not his face from shame, from shame. He hid not his face from shame, from shame and spitting."

The next chapter of the Book of Isaiah begins "Ho". You could win bets on whether or not the word Ho occurs in the Bible though it is widely known that it contains "Ha Ha among the trumpets", which has nothing to do with Alan Clark ha ha ha. The first verse of chapter 55 goes "Ho, every one that thirsteth, come ye to the waters, and he that hath no money; come ye, buy and eat; yea, come, buy wine and milk without money and without price."

It sounds like a recipe for a Euro-MP's life-style.

The polling for this election ended at ten on Thursday night and the count began in the Guild Hall, Abingdon, at nine on Sunday evening. This welcome respite of three days minus one hour passed all too quickly. The time was passed in the following ways.

One: a competition with the cat to see which of us could sleep most in 24 hours. The cat won. By a whisker.

Two: organising a sweepstake on how many votes would be won by the Boston Tea Party.

Three: writing my acceptance speech. "My Lawns, Layers, Gemmemen, Mr Returning Offisher. It is in a spirit of sincere rhubarb that I say to you on this auspish... It has been a fight, a good fight, but a clean fight. I would like to expresh my very sincere platitudes to all concerned. Thank you, from the bottom of my bottom. Good night."

Something along those lines.

Perhaps it was just as well that this speech was not required. In the event the election was won by a pompous man in an exceptionally boring pin-striped suit. Name of Mather. Never cared for him since he put the phone down on me. It should have been won (if not by the BTP) by the Lib Dem Jo Hawkins who in accepting her defeat made a speech of exceptional generosity.

I got 1,018 votes, which I think is quite creditable under the circs, what with being a one-person party that started only a dozen weeks ago. At the same time it would be useless to try to draw a veil over the fact that I got fewer votes than anybody else. Only nine fewer votes than the Natural Law party, though, but then he had the help of yogic flying.

On a different level I think I am entitled to claim a success. If you look at the election results you will see that the national turnout was a percentage in the twenties or low thirties per cent. The Returning Officer told me that in my village it was 51 per cent. Possibly, in this election Aldworth had proportionately the highest turnout anywhere in the country. If that claim turns out to be true, and if this was in any part the result of my efforts, and whether half the village voted for or against me, then I will consider that this entire daft enterprise has been worth while.

Anyway, it's been fun.

LAND OF LOST HORIZONS

It is never pleasant to be the bearer of bad news, but bitter constraint and sad occasion dear compels me now to be one. I just happened to be looking up the telephone number of the Flat Earth Society in what British Telecom calls the Phone Book and I call the telephone directory, when I found that it wasn't there.

I did find someone called B. Flat who lives in London W6, and I hope is a musician at least, if not actually a Recorder. The directory also lists the Flat Centre, and Flat Feet, and the Flat Search Accommodation Agency, followed by such names at Flatau, Flatcher, Flather (a barrister), Flatland and Flatman, but (like Macavity the mystery cat) the Flat Earth Society's not there.

There are various possible explanations for this absence. One is that (not for the first time) British Telecom has made a mistake. Another is that the Flat Earth Society has gone extra-directory. The third possibility, which is almost too dreadful to contemplate but I'm afraid is probably the right one, is that the Flat Earth Society has gone out of existence. Just when we needed it most. There will now be one minute's silence.

(Sixty seconds later.) When I recently let drop the fact that I believe the world to be flat, I was slightly nervous about the possible repercussions. I know from previous experience that stating the plain (or plane) facts can expose a person to derision. Not that I'm complaining. Indeed, I can see that in a way there's a certain justice about it. After all, in our time we laughed at Galileo, we mocked Copernicus, we absolutely hooted at Christopher Columbus. Now it is the turn of the round-earthists to laugh at us. We can take it.

It could have been predicted as easily as the arrival of Halley's comet that my remarks would release a deluge of letters from round-earthists with their crackpot theories. And so they did. Perhaps "deluge" is an exaggeration. There were in fact three letters.

One letter said that when Sir Francis Drake circumnavigated the world, on arrival back at Tilbury the ship's logbook showed that he had lost a day. I can't see that this proves anything other than that Drake was a poor bookkeeper.

Next question, please. How can the world be flat, asks A. Fool of Lostwithiel, when it's quicker to fly to Japan over the Pole? One answer is that you have the prevailing wind behind you. The other is that it depends where you are. If you are flying to Japan from New Zealand a route over the Pole would be irrational even by the standards of round-earthists.

Another answer is supplied in a letter from Mr John Illegible Signature (Sanner? Sannon? Ganner? Gannon?) who points out that, though the earth is obviously flat, it is on a tilt. This is why the great transatlantic liners like the Queen Mary crossed from Southampton to New York in 3½ days but took four days coming back. Once it's pointed out to you, you can see that is is obvious that the return journey is uphill.

Be that as it may, it is surely high time that the quarrel between round-earthists and flat-earthists was brought to an end. I suggest as a compromise that we agree that the earth is neither flat nor spherical. It is slightly curved, like the back of a turtle. Such, I have been told, was the view given to a Western traveller by an Oriental philosopher who said that the world actually stands on the back of the Great Turtle. And what does the Great Turtle stand on? On the back of an even larger turtle. And what, asked the man from the West, does that stand on? "Nice one, mister" replied the wise man, "but it's turtles all the way down."

After which all that remains to be said is that in the coming Fulham by-election there will be candidates standing for the Official Monster Raving Loony Party, the European Democratic Repatriation Party, the Connoisseur

Wine Party, Captain Rainbow's Party, Democratic Rights for Northern Ireland Party, the All-Party Anti-Common Market Party, and the Humanist Party. There are even candidates for the Conservatives, for Labour and the Liberal-SDP Alliance. But is there a Flat Earth Party candidate? There is not. Is this not a sign of the times? It is.

Guardian, *3rd April, 1986.*

KNEES UP CHARLIE BROWN

For as long as anyone can remember the *Guardian* has been running Gary Trudeau's Doonesbury strip. Its evident popularity puzzles me. I rarely understand it, and when I do it seems terribly feeble. Doubtless one of my blind spots. Fortunately Doonesbury is more than made up for by Steve Bell's "If..." which is the best thing since such great strips as Bill Tidy's Fosdyke Saga and Trog's Flook.

For a glorious few years Doonesbury appeared alongside a re-run of Krazy Kat. When the *Guardian* rudely interrupted Krazy without warning, it was to make space for the Sky TV listings. O tempora! O mores! The Deputy Editor at the time was Alan Rusbridger. In reply to my protests he said that he doubted there would be more than two or three letters of complaint. That doesn't sound much but (people outside journalism are always surprised to hear) even two or three letters is quite a lot. Newspapers receive far fewer letters than they like to give the impression they do. When you read about the bulging postbag that some controversial article has provoked it usually turns out to be about eight letters.

So I was being quite bold when I bet Alan a tenner that there would be at least a dozen letters about Krazy Kat's dismissal. Admittedly I wrote quite a few myself, just to be sure, and of course my ruse was rumbled: after all, I was dealing with the Preston-Rusbridger team that was to delight us all by rumbling Neil Hamilton and Jonathan Aitken.

Even so there were more than enough genuine pro-Krazy letters for me to win the bet and Alan, through gritted teeth, paid up. In spite of this, sad to say, my "Bring Back the Kat" campaign came to nothing. I still regret the absence of Krazy six times a week, and in retrospect see the strip's demise as marking the beginning of a change in the character of the *Guardian*. In recent years the paper has had glorious moments (conspicuously the Hamilton and Aitken ones); it remains indispensable and is still a paper I am proud to be associated with, but for better and worse it is not the paper I first wrote for some 35 years ago.

Geo. Herriman's Kat (a cat, originally) first appeared in September 1903. The strip continued with unbounded inventiveness until Herriman died in 1944. In a reversal of the relationships of other comic-strip psychodramas the dog-policman Offissa Pup pines for Krazy Kat who is besotted by the mouse Ignatz who doesn't give a hoot for anyone in Cocorino county — Krazy taking the bonce-bruising bricks hurled by Ignatz as signs of affection ("Li'l dahlink"). The rich dialogue is in a language all of its own, and the backdrops are (along with Little Nemo and the best of Disney) among America's most adventurous contributions to surrealism.

In an essay written in 1963, but which I came across only recently, Umberto Eco (*Apocalypse Postpone*d, BFI, 1994) says that the poetry of Krazy Kat

> originated from a certain lyrical stubbornness in the author, who repeated his tale ad infinitum, varying it always but sticking to his theme. It was thanks only to this that the mouse's arrogance, the dog's unrewarded compassion, and the cat's desperate love could arrive at what many critics felt was a genuine state of poetry, an uninterrupted elegy based on sorrowing innocence.

This is in the course of an essay on Charles M. Schultz's Charlie Brown, which gratifyingly and eloquently shares my admiration for Krazy and Peanuts. Eco sees the poetry in both of them.

I came late to the Kat (and, in fairness, thanks to the *Guardian*). The world of Charlie Brown I had been introduced to long before, in 1963 by a girl in Sweden (thanks, Angela). Five years later the show "You're a good man, Charlie Brown" opened at the Fortune Theatre in London. I was at that time literary editor of *New Society*, and had just bought a capacious leather case. This was an essential piece of equipment for a literary editor in those days. It was used for carrying unwanted review copies to Gaston's, where they gave you half the cover price for whatever you brought in. This was probably a sackable offence but was generally considered a perk of the job, and the practice is (I am told) not unknown among literary editors to this very day.

Shortly before Charlie Brown appeared on the London stage Simon Gray looked in on my office on his way to Mile End where he taught (as I did briefly) at Queen Mary College, the setting of his play *Butley* and the recent short novel *Breaking Hearts*. As we left my office on the way to lunch I commented that Simon had a leather case just like mine. We agreed that it was an excellent sort of case except that, Simon commented, it was so heavy that it felt full even when empty.

After lunch we went our separate ways — Simon to Queen Mary to give a lecture, me back to *New Society* to write about Charlie Brown. Opening my leather case I found that it contained a copy of *Jane Eyre* and notes for a lecture on the Brontës. Even as I was looking at these in bewilderment Simon was beginning his lecture by opening his bag and finding a dozen volumes of Charlie Brown. I don't know what Simon said in his lecture, but (when duly re-united with my collection of the work of Charles M. Schultz) this is what I wrote.

Charlie Brown is worth more than $15 million a year. The strip is followed by 90 million readers a day in a thousand different papers and magazines all over the world. In this country the strip is in the *Observer*, the *Daily Sketch* and *Woman*, and it appears in almost every country in Europe — from *Ilta Sanomat* in Finland, *Politiken* in Denmark,

Expressen in Sweden and *Aftonposten* in Norway to *Figura, L'Unita* and *Paesa Sera* in Italy (Charlie Brown's characteristic exclamation "Good grief!" comes out in Italian as "Misericordia!")

Furthermore, in book form Peanuts — which, for somewhat obscure reasons, is the strip's proper name — has sold more than 20 million copies in the United States alone. A record, "Snoopy and the Red Baron" by a group called the Royal Guardsmen, has sold more than three million copies. A full-length feature film is being made in Hollywood, there have been television programmes, and the show *You're a good man, Charlie Brown* — which opened at the Fortune Theatre in London last week — is already running successfully in six towns in the United States, and a similar show has been on in Stockholm for some months.

Peanuts is, then, a success on the scale of the Beatles and James Bond; and like the Beatles (and unlike Bond) it is a success that, with certain reservations, is deserved. First, the reservations. The strip often repeats itself, and the variations on a basic theme can be flogged to death. Sometimes the strip is insufferably twee, and the sayings of the infant cast are at times not so much funny as merely cute. Then there is the *Reader's Digest*-type "philosophy" and the apparent theological designs that the strip fairly often has on the reader. Charles M. Schulz, the creator of the strip, is himself a lay-preacher in a sect called the "Church of God". A whole book — *The Gospel according to Peanuts* by Robert Short — has been devoted to elucidating the parable aspect of the strip; this book alone has sold some half a million copies in the United States.

The merit of the strip, and what makes one's reservations unimportant, comes from the personalities of the cast. They are a psychically vulnerable lot — all, in one way or another, losers and as packed with neuroses as any of Feiffer's characters.

The hero (or anti-hero) of the strip, Charlie Brown, wears a zig-zag patterned shirt and has a perfectly round head (a characteristic greeting is "Hey there, Charlie

Brown, is that your face or are you hiding behind a balloon?") He is always referred to by his full name, Charlie Brown, never Charlie. He is not as wishy-washy as he thinks he is, and as he is always being told he is. Charlie Brown is a normal human being, kind-hearted, generous and fallible — especially fallible. More than that, he is a failure. He can never get his kite into the air, he always loses baseball games, has never won at checkers. He is depressed, miserable and self-pitying: "Nobody likes me," he says, "I don't have a single friend in the whole world. I can't play baseball, I can't play football, I can't play checkers, I can't do *anything*. I'm a complete flop." Asked where he feels out of place, he replies "Earth". Asked how long he's been depressed, he replies "Six years" (his age).

Rarely are his cosmic woes relieved. A brief moment of happiness came when his baby sister was born. He hears the news on the phone and rushes from the house shouting "I'm a *father!* I mean, my *dad's* a father! *I'm* a brother." His joy is not unconfined for long, for the loathsome Lucy makes the damping comment "I suppose it's never occurred to you that over-population is a serious problem."

Charlie Brown's trouble, like that of all born losers, is that he cannot adjust to the viciousness of life: it comes as a fresh surprise each time. The horrible girls, on the other hand, are perfectly adjusted to it — indeed they are actually part of it. They use Charlie Brown as a butt: "You're *weak*, you're a *jellyfish*, you're *dumb*, you're *stupid*, you're *ignorant* and you have a *silly face*" they say, and walk off leaving Charlie Brown more miserable than ever. Schroeder, passing by, comments "Poor Charlie Brown. I see the cats have been using you to sharpen their claws again, huh?"

Lucy is egotistic, vain, selfish, conceited, treacherous, domineering and a bully. The idea that she may not be universally liked is incomprehensible to her: "Dislike *me*? How could anyone possibly dislike *me*? There's nothing to dislike. Jealous, maybe ... yes, I could understand that ... but dislike? No, that's just not possible."

The only chink in her iron-clad armament is Schroeder: her infatuation for him is never in any way reciprocated. Schroeder's passion, in contrast to the brutally realistic Lucy, is art. On his toy piano he plays classical music with virtuoso fluency. Beethoven's birthday is more important to Schroeder than is his own, and when he whistles for the dog he whistles Beethoven's F minor sonata.

Schroeder's musical ability is, of course, years ahead of the rest of his development. His counterpart and complement is Linus, who is emotionally retarded and intellectually precocious. Linus's problem is security: the only thing that prevents him from tumbling over the brink into psychic chaos is his blanket. Under such circumstances it is understandable that he and his blanket are inseparable. But Linus, in spite of his blanket-holding and thumb-sucking, is the most intellectual and verbally by far the most articulate of the children. "The way I see it," he says, "'the cow jumps over the moon' indicates a rise in farm prices ... the part about the dish running away with the spoon must refer to the consumer. Do you agree with me, Charlie Brown?" "I can't say", Charlie Brown replies, "I don't pretend to be a student of prophetic literature."

There is a small supporting cast of other children, of whom the most intriguing is the unnaturally dirty Pig-pen — "The only person I know," Charlie Brown reflects, "who can get dirty walking in a snowstorm." But the one character in the strip whose importance rivals that of Charlie Brown himself is Snoopy, the dog.

Snoopy is the only dog in the world who worries about his cholesterol level, the only dog that is afraid of spiders, the only dog that gets claustrophobia in long grass, the only dog that tries to get a sun-tan, the only dog that can blush, the only dog that has a van Gogh and a pool-table in his kennel.

Snoopy has as many problems and as many neuroses as any human. He sleeps *on top of* his kennel. But that little quirk is as nothing compared with his identity problem. Snoopy is a dog, yesterday he was a dog, and tomorrow in all probability he will still be a dog. Sometimes he is reconciled to this, even proud of it: "I wonder why some of us were born dogs while others were born people ... is it just pure chance, or what is it? Somehow, the whole thing doesn't seem very fair ... why should *I* have been the lucky one?" But another day he reflects that he is tired of being just a dog "and I'm tired of *associating* with dogs! If I were a human being, I wouldn't even *own* a dog." Lucy, wearing a new coat, tells Snoopy to get away — "you've got dog hair all over you." Snoopy gets away, reflecting "What in the world does she expect, feathers?"

His escapes from the canine condition are various — in sleep, in food, in manic displays of dancing, but mainly in elaborate fantasy. At various times he pretends to be, among other things, a penguin, a vulture, a dinosaur, a pelican, Dracula, a sea-monster, a giraffe, a polar bear, a snake, a gorilla, a rhinoceros, a pirate, a crocodile, a wolf and the captain of a sinking ship.

His favourite fantasy, however, (and it is the most popular with the readers, too) is that he is a First World War fighter pilot. His mortal foe is the Red Baron (who is clearly based on the German air ace Baron von Richthofen — Frieda Lawrence's relative). In the book *Snoopy and the Red Baron* (Holt, Rinehart & Winston), which is devoted entirely to this particular fantasy, Snoopy sits in flying goggles on top of his kennel (transformed in his imagination into a Sopwith Camel). "Here I am flying high over France in my Sopwith 'Camel' searching for the infamous Red Baron! Suddenly anti-aircraft fire begins to burst below my plane..." Invariably the Red Baron outwits him: Snoopy is shot down, falls off his kennel into his supper dish and back to reality. The strip ends with Snoopy shaking his fist and threatening his antagonist: "Someday I'll get you, Red Baron."

Of course he won't, any more than Linus will ever give up his blanket, or Schroeder will ever play rock and roll, or

Charlie Brown will ever get his kite in the air or win a baseball game. The loser Charlie Brown, the insecure Linus, the fantasist Snoopy, the aesthete Schroeder — they are appropriate comic-book heroes for our time — which W.H. Auden has called the Age of Anxiety.

New Society, *8 February, 1968*

BAXTER BASICS

From the outside it looks like any other house in the quiet South London terraced street, but step through the front door (after it's been opened) and you enter the world of Glen Baxter, a world of cowboys, cement-mixers, tight-rope walkers, telescopes, microscopes, textual analysis, Camembert, tweed jackets, pumice, fire-places, art critics, olives, Brenda, intrepid explorers with pith helmets, detectives with magnifying glasses, and a surprising number of gourds.

"Sigmund Freud might have had something to say about the gourds," speculated Boston. That's what happens in the world of Glen Baxter. You find yourself talking in inverted commas, and doing unaccustomed things like speculating. Minutes later I was surmising. Having written the word down it looks odd, as though it was trying to be surprising and something went wrong. To surmise properly you need eagle eyes, like stout Cortez, and be silent upon a peak in Darien, wherever that is.

"I like the word," explained Baxter. "I like its shape," he elaborated. I can't remember if he was talking about gourds or the word written in large capital letters on the wall of his studio: PLÖTZLICH, which is the German for suddenly.

"And Brenda?" Brenda's appearances in the Baxter world are not rare. He once did a drawing for the *New Yorker* which showed some sort of Albanian brigand with fancy boots and gaucho trousers who is defiantly and ferociously placing one foot on a small dark object. The caption was "It soon became apparent that Brenda would not be sharing the meat-ball with us, after all." This came back from the *New Yorker* printers with a note saying "Doesn't look like a Brenda to me."

It was mid-morning, and on television a group of people were talking animatedly. From their mouths came squeaks, trills, shrieks and twitterings. It was bizarre. Not being familiar with day-time television I resolved to watch more of it in future. It was a while before I realised that the sound on the TV had been switched off and just under the set was a tape-recorder playing Australian bird songs. This was disconcerting.

My notes become muddled at this point, which is why what follows may not flow with the seamlessness that the reader has the right to expect. Day-dreaming is an important part of the Baxter process, and watching chat-shows to the sound of Australian bird-song is the kind of thing that helps. Other sources include remarks overheard on the bus or books opened at random.

I asked him whether he thinks of the caption first and then invents an improbable image to go with it, or vice versa. Even as I was speaking I realised that this was probably the most fatuous question I had ever asked anyone in any interview in my entire career, and my apology and retraction came tumbling after. With characteristic suavity Baxter rescued me from my gaffe. He said the song-writer Sammy Kahn had been asked a similar question. Which did he think of first — the melody or the lyrics? Sammy Kahn replied that what he thought of first was the cheque.

Baxter found an early source of day-dreaming at school where he spent hours not really listening to teachers. An exception was a French teacher who wore a pince-nez and had a fob-watch. He was taking them through a Victor Hugo novel. Hardly were they three words into the book when the teacher would jump up and say "That reminds me of a place in Palestine where the tramlines are made of copper because there's a copper-mine nearby..." Every word of Victor Hugo's would start him off on another digression. When the bell rang for end of lesson, the teacher would take out his fob-watch and look at it in total disbelief. By the end of term they hadn't got past the first page, had a most unusual understanding of the works of Victor Hugo and had acquired a vast quantity of random information.

Then there was Biggles. Glen Baxter's brother was a Biggles fan. He remembers an illustration with the caption "Bluejackets faster than Ginger could count". He found this enigmatic, poetic — and it is indeed a metrically perfect pentameter. It's a tiny found poem, part of the surrealism of everyday life which Baxter is adept in detecting.

I had heard about his stammer. Otherwise I doubt if I would have noticed it. In fact it was only really apparent when we discussed it, and at the same time I found myself resurrecting my own vestigial stutter. For Glen Baxter as a child it was a real impediment. He would avoid certain words which he knew were going to terrify him. He would find Byzantine ways of getting round words he was afraid of. This might mean that he went into a shop and came out having bought something which was easy to say but not what he wanted.

There were words that he would envisage. Difficult ones to be avoided. And words he liked. Gourd, for example, and PLÖTZLICH. His books have been translated into many languages. Finnish, for example. In Finnish *The Impending Gleam* is called *Outo Hohto,* which sounds Japanese. Baxter turned over the pages and read out the Finnish captions. "The *Impending Gleam* is funnier in Finnish," mused Baxter. He would probably write all his books in Finnish if he spoke the language. You can see his point. Finnish is an essentially Baxterish language. Like Hungarian. And Japanese.

What is the tiny difference between those things that are funny and those that are not? He tells me that Joseph Heller's novel was originally called *Catch-18*. Bob Gottlieb changed it to *Catch-22*. It's immediately obvious that *Catch-22* is better, but why? *Snow White and the Six Dwarfs?* It doesn't work.

It's hard to dissect humour without murdering it, but the French are brave and I have a catalogue for a Baxter exhibition a year ago in Caen, with an introduction by Jacques Meunier (who, just by the way, is an unfrocked ethnologist and a novice star-gazer, or so he says). Meunier explains that Baxter's is "l'humour anglais". It is deadpan *(humour grave et rire plat)*, and involves understatement *(impassibilité, litote, laconisme et sous-estimation des situations)* and is also self-mocking *(ironie de soi)*.

At art school in Leeds Baxter was a Cubist. In the early Sixties he went through all the -isms. While he wanted to do surrealism the teachers imposed a regime of American abstract painting which he calls Stalinist (the regime or American abstract painting?). He wrote short stories and poetry. He mentions John Ashbery's poems. I say I find Ashbery's poems impenetrable and a slight hesitation on the word prompts Baxter to say simultaneously "Impeccable". So we bat impenetrable and impeccable between us, and I decide to give Ashbery another go, which is more than any literary critic has ever persuaded me to do.

He finished art school with a diploma painting called "A ventriloquist's waiting room". Then he got a job teaching football and pottery in Leytonstone. He liked the idea of Leytonstone because it is where Alfred Hitchcock was born and he thought it might be interesting. It wasn't. He spent two blissful years there before going on to teach in Islington, and then at Goldsmith's. He wrote more short stories and poems, and admired Apollinaire and Frank O'Hara, poets amongst painters. His work appeared in the *London Magazine* and in New York, at the Institute of Contemporary Arts and then regularly in the *Observer*.

He has published about ten books, which have been translated into countless languages. He is biggest in France. In a deli in Pluckemin, New Jersey, he is a sandwich: a Baxter is hot corned beef, horse-radish, cheese and slaw. Unexpected as it is to be a sandwich he has never thought of himself as a cartoonist. He does pictures with captions (like Magritte in "This is not a pipe"). When he's travelling and the person in the next seat asks what he does he says "I'm in the paint business," or "I travel in trousers."

I mention Krazy Kat and he says "Now we're being serious". This pleases me for I consider Krazy Kat to be like the Chevalier Bayard — *"sans reproche"*.

At this point my notes say "France and America are different." How true. How very true.

He shows me a Baxter bibliography he has compiled. I study it and try to spot which ones he has made up. Sir Arthur Beverley Baxter, *The Blower of Bubbles*. Eric Baxter, *The Study Book of Coal*. Sir George Washington Baxter, *Elk Hunting in Sweden*. Hamilton A. Baxter, *Blood Histamine Levels in Swine Following Total Body X-Radiation and a Flash Burn*. Dow Vawter Baxter, *Importance of Fungi* and *Defects in Handling Airplane Spruce*.

Fred Baxter, *Snake for Supper*. Allan Muir Baxter, *The Distribution of Load along Nuts; The Fatigue of Bolts and Studs*. Thomas Richard Baxter, *Caribbean Bishops*. Brian Newland Baxter, *Teach Yourself Naval Architecture*. Thomas Preston Nowell Baxter, *Lomelines — an Address to the members of the Girls' Friendly Society*.

He swears they are all real, and when challenged was usually able to take from his shelves a copy of the book. Still, one has to check one's facts and I could see that I would have to trek to the British Museum and trawl through the British Library catalogue. Such was the plan which Baxter and Boston had in mind as they sallied forth in a northerly direction. Quite what went wrong is hard to determine but the intrepid pair ended up having lunch in Soho, followed by a visit to the National Gallery, where Baxter pointed out a transparent dog in the Verrochio. "Going round the National Gallery with Glen Baxter is an unusual experience," reflected Boston.

Guardian, *26th November, 1996*.

BOLOGNA

In the summer of 1974 twelve people were killed by a bomb on the "Italicus" express train near Bologna. It was six years before eight neo-fascists were sent for trial. Just two days later, on 2 August 1980, Italy's annual summer holiday mass exodus from the cities was beginning. The waiting-room at Bologna station was crowded when at 10.25 in the morning a suitcase containing 90 pounds of high explosives detonated, leaving a crater 5 foot deep, 85 dead and some 200 wounded.

On a wall in an inconspicuous corner of the station, next to the McDonald's, a simple memorial says "2 Agosto 1980 *Vittime de terrorismo fascista*," "2 August 1980 Victims of Fascist Terrorism." This is followed by the names and ages of 85 men, women and children.

> Francesco Cesare Diomede Fresa aged 14
> Errica Frigeria in Diomede Fresa 57
> Vito Diomede Fresa 62
> Luca Mauri 6
> Anna Maria Bosio in Mauri 28
> Carlo Mauri 32
> Manuela Gallon 11
> Natalia Agostini in Gallon 40
> Marina Trolese 16
> Anna Maria Salvagnini in Trolese 51
> Roberto de Marchi 21
> Elisabetta Manea in de Marchi 60

So the list goes on, and on, the names and ages revealing with terrible clarity the identities and relationships of the murdered infants, children and adolescents; the adults, young, middle-aged and old; the boys and girls, brothers and sisters, sons and daughters, parents, grandparents, friends, lovers, some travelling alone, some in groups, whole families, with ages from 3 to 86.

Bologna station is a dignified but unpretentious piece of architecture, well-suited to a town which is notable for its decorum rather than its decoration (though photographs of the vanished waiting-room suggest it was magnificent). I have been through the station a number of times over the last ten years without paying it much attention. It was just a place to arrive at or leave from. When I first heard that its future was the subject of a huge row I was puzzled, as Desdemona must have been when the Moor made such a fuss about a handkerchief. Certainly it was a very fine handkerchief: an Egyptian gave it to Othello's mother, there was magic in the web of it and the worms were hallowed that did breed the silk. A very fine handkerchief indeed, but it isn't really the handkerchief that it's all about, as Othello knows, as Iago knows, as we know, as everyone except poor Desdemona knows.

Bologna station was built in the style of a Florentine palazzo by Gaetano Ratti in 1871. After more than a century it needs modernising and enlarging to cope with the demands of local and regional transport, and to play its key role in the national and European network. All roads may go to Rome, but its geographical position in the Italian peninsula means that all roads (and railways) go through Bologna.

In 1983 the Communist *Sindaco* (Mayor) of Bologna, Renato Zangheri, announced a competition for a design for a new station which would at the same time be a memorial to the victims of the Fascist bomb. Five plans emerged, after which nothing happened. Then at the beginning of 1994 the Italian State Railways, (FS, *Le ferrovie dello Stato*) announced plans for a number of stations for its new high-speed network. None of the architects was Italian. The one appointed for Bologna was the Catalan architect Ricardo Bofill. The Bologna Council *(Comune)* supported this scheme, proposing to build a new station and develop the environs on a joint fifty-fifty basis with FS. This meant the end of the Zangheri competition, and the five chosen architects accordingly sued for damages.

Initial opposition to the new scheme in general snowballed when the plans of the neo-modernist Bofill were revealed. Urban conservationists were predictably dismayed at the idea of the 21st century making such a brash intrusion into the medieval city with a scheme conspicuous for its glass, steel and concrete, topped by two huge towers which brought to mind the words sore, thumb and stick out.

If FS could call in a big-name foreign architect, so too could defenders of the old station. Enter Leon Krier, a traditionalist who has been an adviser and close associate of the Prince of Wales, for whom he produced the masterplan for Charles's Poundbury development in Dorset. The Prince himself has shown an active interest in the conservation of Italian cities, and has twice opened architecture conferences in Bologna on the theme of urban renewal. He hasn't actually refurbished his monstrous carbuncle speech in Italian, but it's waiting in the wings, and whereas in Britain having Charles on your side could be seen as a liability and an embarrassment, in Italy his architectural views are treated with respect.

The Bologna *comune* has been in Communist hands ever since the war, and anything it does is opposed by the Right. The Berlusconi-owned newspaper *Il Giornale* has consistently attacked the Bofill scheme. But this is not simply a battle between the left and right, or of traditionalists and modernists. There is plenty of room for positions in the middle for those who don't see it in either/or terms. Suppose that Bofill has produced a design that is excellent in itself but not right for Bologna, or for a railway station. The Bofill camp may see it as the right building in the right place, but others might think it is a good scheme but in the wrong place, or the right place but a bad scheme, or simply the wrong building in the wrong place. All of these viewpoints recognise the importance of the context, historical, political, economic, social, architectural and Bolognese.

* * *

Bologna *la Dotta, la Grassa, la Rossa*. From the 13th century Bologna has been known as the Learned, the Fat, the Red. Red in the colour of its buildings and its politics. Fat in prosperity and the best food in Italy, both in cooking and produce, with its profusion of sausages, hams, salami, mortadella, cheese, confectionery and pasta. Bologna's tortellini are literally divine since their shape is modelled on the navel of Venus. The world-famous ice-cream machines come from Bologna, and the coffee is unsurpassed. How they make it so strong I have no idea. *Nessun dorma,* indeed.

Bologna the Learned, because it has the oldest university in Europe, perhaps in the world (China has its claim). Martial called the Roman Bononia (Bologna) *"culta"* in the 1st century AD. The *Studium* was supposedly founded in 1088. The university pioneered the study of medicine and gave degrees to women in the 18th century, a couple of hundred years before British universities did. Thomas à Becket studied here, and so did Copernicus, Luther, Dante, Petrarch, Boccaccio, Erasmus, Ariosto, Carducci and Bassani. Bologna produced Galvani, Marconi, Fermi, the Maserati car-making brothers (with Ferrari and Lamborghini just down the road), the Carracci family of painters, Guido Reni, the Bolognese school and Giorgio Morandi. To music Bologna and its region have given Verdi, Rossini, Respighi, Toscanini and Pavarotti. We owe Bologna our calendar (Pope Gregory XIII) and radio (Gugliemo Marconi).

Bologna is extraordinary not for any one particular building but all of them together, the place as a whole. What provides its unique and lovely cohesiveness is the *portici* (arcades). Bologna had arcades in the 3rd century BC, but they only became general in the 12th century. The 10,000 students of the university created a housing problem which was not easily solved in the confines of a walled city. The *comune* ruled that buildings should have rooms built out projecting over the street. These were supported with props made first of wood (some of which survive), then columns of brick or stone, joined by arches — the result, arcades. Every street had arcades on both sides, with a minimum height that allowed the passage of a man on a horse. The owners of the houses had the responsibility of maintaining the arcades in front of them for public use.

The evolution of the arcades is a perfect example of form following function. No one said "Arcades would look nice; now what shall we do with them?" which is the kind of thinking (lack of) that critics note in the Millenium Dome, and the Bofill plan imposed on Bologna by FS in Rome. The 12th century communal ruling about arcades is as enlightened and civic-minded a piece of town-planning anywhere. The result is that Bologna has 35 kilometres of arcades, more than any other city in the world (even Rome under Augustus boasted only 20 kilometres). What canals are to Venice, what fountains, little squares and courtyards are to Aix-en-Provence, what Regency crescents and terraces are to Bath, the arcades are to Bologna.

They make street life pleasant all the year round, providing a pedestrian sanctuary, a shelter from the rain and snow in winter, and shade in summertime when the temperature is regularly up in the eighties. The arcades and the size of the city make walking the natural way to get about. The town goes at walking pace, *andante,* neither quick nor slow but fluently, making a welcome contrast to the hectic, asphyxiating, noisy and noisome *prestissimo* of other great cities. It is as agreeable a city as any I know, and its architecture belongs to a different world from that of imposing structures such as St Peter's in Rome or Mitterrand's *grands projets* — or Ricardo Bofill's plan for the new station.

Bologna *la Rossa,* the Red. Red in bricks and terracotta and the earth colours of its walls, and red in its political affiliation. The anti-clericalism of Emilia-Romagna goes back to its time as one of the Papal States. In the nineteenth century socialists and anarchists proliferated, and in 1919 socialists polled 60 per cent of the vote. Bologna suffered severely in the struggle against Fascism and Nazism. Thousands of Resistance partisans were killed in the war, and the German reprisals of Major Walter Reder's SS battalion were dreadful. The "march of death" which began in August 1944 when 560 men and women were killed in Sant'Anna di Stazzema ended two months later when in the village of Marzabotto, fifteen miles from Bologna, the Nazis murdered 1,830 men, women and children. Bologna was one of the few cities that liberated itself. When President Scalfaro opened the Morandi museum four years ago he added "the heroic" to Bologna's epithets.

The post-war Italian Communist leader Palmiro Togliatti told a Bologna audience in 1946 that "The torpor which seems to reign elsewhere is absent here... one notes a pride and satisfaction absent elsewhere". Bologna has had a Communist administration since the war. Apart from Kerala in India it is perhaps the only place in the world where Communists have won and held power through free elections, and like Kerala it has the reputation of being the best administered, most socially progressive and egalitarian, and least corrupt place in the country.

Bologna-style Communism never had Stalinist leanings but subtly mixed ideology with pragmatism. Its achievements are all the more remarkable in that they have been in the face of hostility from the national Christian Democrat governments, which have been notably incompetent and corrupt, subservient to the United States in a way markedly different from the "Red Belt"'s refusal to kowtow to Moscow. In 1964 Togliatti said the Bologna model was "a civic cohabitation of a higher kind, in which new forms of content, of understanding and of working together are established in the interests of all working people." It has been reformist while acting inside the capitalist system. Paul Ginsborg says in his *History of Con-*

temporary Italy that "If there is a single, recurrent, almost obsessive theme in the political history of post-war Italy, it is the need for reform and the failure to achieve it." That remains true, and Bologna and its province remain an exception.

In the Sixties and Seventies people came from all over the world to study Bologna's town planning, its primary schools, its cheap (even free) public transport, its welfare for old people and health care. To take one example, whereas in Rome public housing was about 8 per cent of what was built in the 60s, in Bologna it was more than a third. In most Italian cities (Rome and Venice, for example) the working population after the war was pushed to the outskirts while restored houses were rented or sold to the wealthy. In Bologna the centre was kept for the working people, the policy being to concentrate on "active preservation". Old houses in the historical centre were renovated for public housing. Modern building was confined almost entirely to suburbs such as Bolognina and the Fiera district which has staged innumerable trade fairs. This area with its towers by the Japanese architect Kenzo Tange looks to me like a Dystopia dreamed up by Jacques Tati, but like them or not these buildings are remote from the medieval town in distance as well as style. With Bofill's scheme they would be brought geographically together, and collide.

Italian street-maps give an account of locally respected historical events and cultural and political figures. The cosmopolitan names of Bologna's streets and squares include (plus, of course, quantities of saints) Albinoni, Aldo Moro, Salvador Allende, Balzac, Beethoven, Caravaggio, Canaletto, Cellini, Cefalonia, Cherubini, Chopin, Cimabue, Collodi, Copernicus, Corelli, Croce, d'Annunzio, Dante, Darwin, Dickens, Donatello, Donizetti, Alessandro Fleming, Yuri Gagarin, Galileo, Galvani, Gandhi, Garibaldi, Gogol, Gramsci, Independence, Martin Luther King, Lenin, Leopardi, Liberation, Lidice, Lincoln, Machiavelli, Carlo Marx, Marconi, Maserati, Enrico Mattei, Matteotti, Mazzini, Modigliani, Morandi, Mozart, Neruda, Isacco Newton, Pasteur, Pirandello, Poe, Puccini, Republic, Resistance, Risorgimento, Roosevelt, Rossini, Sacco and Vanzetti, Spartacus, Stalingrad, Stendhal, Italo Svevo, Togliatti, Tolstoy, Unity, Verdi and Volta.

In front of the station is the Piazza Medaglie d'Oro, for the gold medals won by Bologna for its sacrifices in the war. At the other end of the via dell'Indipendenza is the Piazza Maggiore, where a huge wall is covered with thousands of framed black-and-white photographs of resistance fighters and others killed by the Germans. Another memorial is to the thousands more of the "Acqui" Mountain Infantry Division killed in Corfu and Cefalonia. These are the young Italian soldiers about whom Louis de Bernières writes in *Captain Corelli's Mandolin*. The memorial gives the numbers of those killed in combat, and then the much larger numbers of those shot by the Germans.

Pisa is famous for its leaning tower. Bologna has two leaning towers. They arouse affectionate feelings that complement the emotions felt in front of the memorials in the Piazza Maggiore. Stendhal said that a Bolognese far from home could burst into tears just by thinking about his beloved towers. These architectural curiosities are at the point from which the streets of the city radiate, and they are the landmark of Bologna.

The *due torri* (two towers) were built in 1119. The Asinelli is 98 metres high, only a metre less than the campanile of St Mark's in Venice, and is a metre out of true. Dante mentions its neighbour, the Garisenda, which in his time was the higher of the two, but it was unsafe and in 1360 its height was reduced to 48 metres. Though now shorter than its partner it leans even more, being 3.2 metres out. The towers lurch towards one another in a way which has reminded travel-writers of two drunks propping each other up, but from some angles they make up a heroically two-fingered V for victory.

The two towers are the very symbol of Bologna. This makes it tactless of the Catalan architect Ricardo Bofill to have put two towers on top of his plan for the new station. (Faulty towers, one can't help thinking, and he comes from Barcelona). Two towers of glass and steel and concrete and, at 120 metres, head and shoulders over the *due torri* on the Bologna skyline.

Bologna once had many towers; probably not the 200 that guidebooks like to claim, but remains of about 40 still exist. It must have bristled with towers, like San Gimignano where even now 14 of 72 survive. What were they for? If they were look-outs, why need so many? They would have been of little use defensively. An attacker could simply light a fire at the bottom, or bolt the door and let the inhabitants starve. Probably they were built just in a spirit of rivalry. If a Ghibelline put up something high, then a Guelph had to go higher. Militarily it's called an arms race; domestically it's keeping up with the Joneses. Putting a bell as high up as possible makes it audible for a long way but these are not bell-towers. In Manhattan and Hong Kong there is a limited amount of land available for building, so it makes sense to build high. Such conditions do not prevail in Bologna or most other places where there are towers.

There is rarely a rational, functional need for towers. Usually their point is their sheer pointlessness. This is as true of the Eiffel Tower as of the Colossus of Rhodes. The Book of Genesis describes the first high-rise. "And they said, let us build us a city and a tower, whose top may reach unto heaven... And the Lord came down to see the city and the tower, which the children of men builded. And the Lord said, Behold, the people is one, and they have all one language; and this they begin to do: and now nothing will be restrained from them, which they have imagined to do. Go, let us go down, and there confound their language, that they may not understand one another's speech." Accordingly he sent the people all off in different directions speaking different languages. The place was called Babel.

In that case building high was motivated by hubristic ambition. In William Golding's *The Spire* it comes from religious mania. In Ibsen's *The Master Builder* it is sex. Solness takes pride in, and the women adore, his erections. The besotted Hilde exclaims to Solness that "It was marvellous — terribly exciting. I couldn't believe any builder in the world could have built such an enormously high tower." She is disappointed to hear that Solness is now building homes for people. She asks "Couldn't you try putting some kind of tower on them too? I mean... something pointing... right up into the air. With a weathercock on top at a great dizzy height."

Solness muses a little: "Strange you should say that. That's what I want to do more than anything." He cheers them both up by saying that the house he's building for himself does have a tower.

> *Hilde:* A high tower?
> *Solness:* Yes.
> *Hilde:* Very high?
> *Solness:* People are sure to say it's too high. For a house.
> *Hilde:* I'll be out first thing in the morning to see that tower.

The ending is most satisfying. Solness climbs his own tower, falls off and is killed.

Closer to Bologna and Bofill is Vitaliano Brancati's *Gli anni perduti (The Lost Years)*. In this serio-comic novel the dynamic outsider Buscaino forms his plan for the sleepy Sicilian town of Nataca (Catania?) before he has set foot in it. He does so even as he catches his first glimpse of Nataca from the train window, and in language that anticipates some of Bofill's comments about Bologna. "'What a town!' he thought. 'All the houses like little flat boxes... Nothing upstanding... Oh, bless the skyscrapers! They may be as arrogant and spiky and hideous as you please, but they speak of a city on its feet, a city wide awake, a city ready and willing to march towards infinity," He scribbles himself a note: "Must stop in Nataca for a couple of months, set up committee then Limited Company. By spring, tower should be built, so in June, back to America. Hurrah for life!" In the head-on collision between dynamism and slothful inertia, the eventual triumph of Sicilian indolence is inevitable.

Another dynamic tower-builder is to be found in Ayn Rand's *The Fountainhead*, a title which gives clear warning of the phallic orientation. Howard Roark (based on Frank Lloyd Wright) is a sort of Nietzschean superman. Admirers of the novel (and they exist) gloss over, or forget, or sublimate, the fact that Roark is a rapist. Not only that, but the heroine's infatuation with Roark comes from his raping of her. The novel is preposterous but it is helpful in any attempt to understand the psychopathology of tower-building.

If that is difficult in all cases (and not just for anti-modernists) it is especially so with Bologna railway station. Glass towers are wrong in Bologna because: one, they are the wrong material in a city of red brick; two, being of glass they will be difficult and costly to keep warm in winter and cool in summer; three, because they are arrogantly taller than the *due torri*, and showing off is not the Bologna way.

The towers are wrong not only in the context of Bologna but also of railway stations. Like the bicycle, the car and the train, stations have evolved a form which is proper to them. Early stations used familiar types, and there are nineteenth-century stations that look like town halls, cathedrals and castles. Union Station, Chicago, is a Roman bath; Slough station is a French château. New, distinctive, modern styles developed as architecture and engineering met in such stations as the Saint Lazare celebrated by Monet, Eiffel's Budapest and Brunel's stations at Paddington, Bristol and elsewhere. Most extraordinary of all is Lewis Cubitt's King's Cross, which is a total anachronism. It was built in 1852 and looks as though it's about a century later, looking as confidently to the future as the neighbouring St Pancras looks back to a pre-railway past.

King's Cross is the forerunner of the clean, direct, modernist architecture that London Underground developed in the 20th century. Charles Holden's 1932 Arnos Grove station with its horizontal front and cylindrical hall boldly states the function of the building and at the same time refers explicitly to the London Underground logo. In Pevsner's *Outline of European Architecture*, which starts with the Parthenon, Arnos Grove is the very last named building. Pevsner says that London Underground stations "became the most perfect examples in London of the style of today, serviceable, uncompromisingly modern, and yet in keeping with the quiet distinction of the Georgian brick house."

Pevsner's comment emphasises the point that different styles can live together, as King's Cross and St Pancras do. If Bologna has to have a new station a Quinlan Terry pastiche is not called for. Nicholas Grimshaw's thrilling Waterloo station shows what can be done. The station tower that disfigures Montparnasse shows how not to do it, and Paris has rebelled successfully against similar projects for the Gare de Lyon and the Gare du Nord where old and new have been successfully integrated.

The commissions for the new Italian stations have all been given to architects of the neo-modernist international style, a style which is apparently not sufficiently flexible to reflect the character and culture of such areas as Lombardy, Tuscany and Piedmont that the railway passes through. Sant'Elia drew Futurist stations (never built) that look Italian. Bofill's plan doesn't look anything. If he had come up with something as crazy as the buildings of Barcelona's Gaudi at least it would be fun. Instead he offers a glass fortress with two featureless towers. Perhaps not plain ugly, like Canary Wharf, and without the affectation of a broken (Chippendale) pediment à la AT&T building, but also without the thrilling Italian stylishness of Nervi and Gio Ponti's Pirelli Centre in Milan. Just plain old filing cabinets, any height you like as long as it's a rectangle. For goodness sake, Bofill's towers don't even lean.

The "Bird" station at Satolas outside Lille is by Bofill's fellow-Catalan Santiago Calatrava. I've never seen it but from photographs it looks exciting. The trouble is that a bird flies while trains are earthbound. They may jump valleys and bore through mountains but they must respect the geographical contours. The gradients of railways are so small they are virtually horizontal. Towers are vertical, and do not speak railway stations.

Like Howard Roark in Ayn Rand's novel, Ricardo Bofill is not an academic. Having failed to complete his professional training at Barcelona he did so again at Geneva. And like Roark he has colossal self-esteem and what looks like contempt for anyone else. He has reacted to criticism of his Bologna scheme in tones of lese-majesty. He has been quoted as saying in the Bologna context that it is dangerous to let the popular will decide, and that "In these cases the elite decides and the people follow" (*La Repubblica* 17 Jan 97). Bologna risks decline, he says. It will become a little city without competitiveness; the economy of Bologna, its part in the next century, will be finished. He echoes, in short, the dynamic tower-builders of the novels of Brancati and Ayn Rand.

David Mackay (*Contemporary Architects* 3rd edition) speaks of Bofill's "fresh amateur approach to architecture and his surprising nonchalance about details and finishes, sadly reflected in the rather fragile durability and weathering of his buildings... the joints of his buildings and the joining of different materials are often crude and primitive"

Bofill is seen as a brilliant showman and self-promoter. "Bofill's own explanations of his work should be treated with care as they are generally tactical and meant for the gallery" says Mackay. Kenneth Frampton in *Modern Architecture* is equally hostile. He hurls at Bofill such phrases and epithets as brutally kitsch classicism, stupefying rhetoric, reactionary identification with the state, worldly success, kitsch romanticism, narcissism, high fashion and flamboyant personality.

Attacks are as much on Bofill the man as Bofill the architect. A recent article in *Il Resto del Carlino* (Bologna's daily newspaper) devotes much of its first paragraph to describing Bofill's cigar and double-breasted blue jacket. Mackay says Bofill "has managed to get his ideas built, first through family backing, then later through agile and persuasive political manoeuvring, disarming the opposition through personal charm, artistic conviction and hard teamwork."

Bofill has certainly not been denied worldly success, with international awards galore and countless prestigious projects. An admiring article by Hugh Broughton (*Building Design* 1995) calls Bofill one of the "elite group whose personalities and activities lift them beyond the realms of normal professional practice into something approaching cult status... Architect of ground-breaking schemes from Barcelona to Chicago and from Paris to Tokyo, he is also a vocal contributor to Catalan politics and the star of a television commercial for yoghourt." Whatever one thinks of ground breaking and yoghurt, Broughton's comments are revealing and since it hasn't been easy to find favourable ones it is only fair to quote them at some length. He says that "Architects tend to react strongly against Bofill's work. This is very encouraging. Architecture needs to be enlivened by flamboyant personalities creating bold statements on a grand scale... This is not an architecture providing a polite contextual approach but an opportunity for Ricardo Bofill's multinational clients (and no doubt himself) to make a mark on the world... As long as this approach is only adopted by an elite group of architects, then it must be good for the image of a profession all too often lacking in real glitz or a sense for the outrageous... It is planning on a heroic scale, carving through industrial sprawl to reinvigorate this historic and industrial city."

Whether it is desirable that architects and their clients should make a mark on the world at the expense of everyone else is at least questionable. It sounds rather like a dog going round lifting its leg against lamp-posts. Perhaps it is, with skyscrapers for lamp-posts.

Bureaucracy, indolence and corruption have such a paralysing effect on Italian politics that it comes to many almost as a relief when the vacuum is filled by a condottiere, a Duce, a man of action (that there is another, democratic way of getting things done is something that Bologna has had the effrontery to show). The classic postwar example was Enrico Mattei. After the war he was put in charge of AGIP, the state petrol company. Since AGIP had no petrol, Mattei's job was to wind up the company. Instead he exploited the discovery of methane gas in the Po valley and built an empire, boasting that in doing so he had broken 8,000 ordinances and laws. A Mayor would wake up in the morning to find that during the night someone had cut a deep trench right through the town. He would protest furiously, Mattei would apologise profusely and fill in the trench — with a pipe-line at the bottom of it. Riding rough-shod over everyone Mattei diversified into petrochemicals, roads, engineering, textiles and nuclear power. He had his own newspaper, *Il Giorno,* and conducted negotiations on equal terms with foreign governments. More than anyone he is credited with the economic miracle that transformed Italy from an impoverished country to one of the wealthiest in the world, claiming by 1986 to have a higher GDP than the United Kingdom, and to be the fifth largest industrial nation in the Western world after the USA, Japan, West Germany and France.

Lorenzo Necci, the chairman of the State Railways (FS) is seen by some to have been in the Mattei mould. He has worked hard to integrate Italian railways into the high-speed network that will link Seville to Malmö, London to Vienna. In Italy it will cut the journey from Bologna to Rome from 147 minutes to 110, and save 1 hour 23 minutes off the present 4 hours 18 minutes to Naples.

In a country forever threatening to fragment, the railways are a truly national organisation and as their 21st century supremo Necci was set to become a very great man indeed. Then last September the front pages of the newspapers showed him in handcuffs on the way to jug, accused with various associates of bribery, peculation, abuse of office, corruption and cooking the books *(falso in bilancio)*.

Bofill was Necci's appointee and Necci's arrest was a setback to the Bofill supporters and a boost to the opposition. An opinion poll showed 81 per cent of Bologna against knocking down the old station, 75 per cent against anything higher than the existing buildings, and almost everyone in favour of a public competition to choose the best scheme. A competition is seen as a safeguard against the corrupt rake-offs and fixing of contracts *(tangentopoli)* which the judicial *Mani Puliti* (clean hands) have cracked down on, bringing about the downfall of people such as Necci and the former Prime Minister Andreotti.

By Italian and EU law a competition must be held for projects over a certain size, but the Mayor of Bologna is totally opposed. He told me in May that it would produce a "Harlequin" scheme and that it would hold everything up. These objections are scornfully dismissed by the Bologna architect Gabriele Tagliaventi, who last year produced for the Department of the Environment the winning scheme for the Marsham Street development in Westminster. Drawing on that experience Tagliaventi reckons that a competition could take six months. He further points out that competitions are normal everywhere, including the former Communist countries, and says that from the First World War to today there have been only two countries which have shown an aversion to architectural competitions: Nazi Germany and modern Italy. He envisages a great competition with architects coming to Bologna from all over the world. It would transform a scandal into an event of great cultural richness.

Tagliaventi is a leading member of the Prince of Wales's A Vision of Europe group, and is associated with the activities in Italy of the Task Force about which Charles speaks in his uniquely toe-curling manner: "I have always regarded my Institute's Summer School as a little army of creation set against the still active armies of destruction which go on threatening the towns and cities of Europe." The effect of such words is to make me at least want to rush off and join the barbarians instanter. Which is a pity. And a nuisance. The fact is that from time to time it may happen that you find yourself holding an opinion even if it means agreeing with the Prince.

Tagliaventi can hardly be blamed for turning to advantage the royal patronage. When up against the forces of the State Railway, the Mayor of the city, and the cigar-toting yoghurt salesman, you need any help you can get.

Tagliaventi is the opposite of a tower-building architect. He likes to pull towers down. If towers were beanstalks he would be Jack the Giant-killer. He is the architect as Samson, pulling down the pillars of the Temple. Towers for Tagliaventi are what windmills were for Don Quixote: their sole purpose is to be tilted at.

Just 25 years ago there was a defining moment in architectural history. In 1955 a worker-housing estate called Pruitt-Igoe opened in St Louis. The award-winning design was by Minoru Yamasaki, architect of the World Trade Centre. This rapidly turned into a slum. After millions of dollars, countless meetings and task-force projects, the residents were asked for suggestions. And they answered with one voice "Blow it... UP! Blow it... UP! Blow it.. UP!" As Tom Wolfe tells the story in *From Bauhaus to Our House,* "The next day the task force thought it over. The poor buggers were right. It was the only solution. In July of 1972, the city blew up the three central blocks of Pruitt-Igoe with dynamite."

Since then many other high-rise buildings have been pulled down: some, such as our own Ronan Point, have self-destructed. Tagliaventi's glossy architecture and town-planning magazine *A and C* (Arches and Columns) gleefully lists the latest skyscrapers to bite the dust — Lyon, Liverpool, Glasgow... the list is impressive. Tagliaventi's personal hit-rate is high. His prize-winning plan for rebuilding an area of

Brussels levelled one skyscraper, and his Marsham Street plan in Westminster knocks out three real stinkers.

Other opponents of the Bofill scheme include Pier Luigi Cervelatti, the master-mind of the post-war restoration of public housing of the historic inner city of Bologna. He has called the new scheme a blow to the heart of the city, a mastadon, an empty shell, a fossil, old and useless before it's built, suicidal and megalomaniac. Giuseppe Campos Venuti is the author of the conservationist and decentralising Regulatory Plan intended to keep housing in the city and traffic and new offices out. He sees the new station which includes FS offices, a hotel, a supermarket and exhibition hall as having precisely the opposite effect.

Public meetings were held with the support of such as Tagliaventi, Cervelatti and Campos Venuti. Polemics raged in the papers. In April last year they began collecting signatures calling for a Referendum. This required the signatures of 5,000 people whose names are on the electoral register. Without the backing of a political or any other kind of organisation this was quite a job, but they set up stalls in the streets and public places and the signatures were collected.

The referendum took place in January and asked three questions. Keep the old station? No new buildings in the area higher than existing ones? An international public competition for any new scheme? The result was what we call a fiasco and the Italian newspapers (in an interesting linguistic exchange) called *uno flop*. More than 60 per cent voted against the FS-*Comune* (Bofill) scheme. On the other hand only 37 per cent of the population voted, which did not achieve the necessary 50 per cent for a quorum that would give the result any force. This low turn-out is not so surprising considering that the Mayor and his Council had actively opposed the Referendum and had urged people not to vote and there had been virtually no support (if not outright opposition) from any political party. Furthermore only a third of the polling stations were opened, and some of these were submerged in voting slips while others were short of them.

Mayor Vitali has somehow interpreted the Referendum as a vote of confidence in him, Bofill and Bologna 2000 (the property company set up jointly by the *Comune* and the State Railways). But since the Referendum other problems have arisen. Elio Garzillo, Superintendent of the Cultural Ministry, has done the equivalent of slapping a preservation order on the old station. When I met Vitali in May he waved aside mention of Garzillo as a mere functionary but Garzillo is proving a hard nut to crack. And then there is the problem of money. The question is whether in the end there's enough for the scheme to go through.

Meanwhile Bofill's behaviour has been very odd. He is clearly piqued at the fact that nobody likes his towers. (It is possible to find people to defend them, but people who are actually enthusiastic about the towers are as rare as hen's teeth). Bofill has responded with new plans. A plan with smaller towers. A plan with *no towers*. He'll keep the old station, but behind a glass wall (why not get Mr and Mrs Christo to wrap it in brown paper and tie it up in a parcel with string?). Bofill's flexibility calls in doubt more than anything the need for the towers. One Bologna architect commented of Bofill's willingness to change his plan that it is as though a surgeon said that what you need is a heart transplant but he'll give you a by-pass if you prefer. Another suggested that it was like Leonardo being prepared to negotiate the number of disciples at the Last Supper.

In June Bofill unveiled his umpteenth plan. He's now lopped 30 metres off the towers. At 90 metres they are now a tactful eight metres shorter than the taller of the *due torri*. They've come down but they're still there. No one's had an ear bitten off yet. The fight goes on.

Guardian, *July 19th, 1997*

STOP PRESS. The Italian Government, under Romano Prodi (himself from Bologna) finally ruled that the old station could be knocked down. However, on October 10th, 1997, Prodi's government fell, thereby symbolically backing the earthquake whcih did such terrible damage to Assisi. Unlike Assisi, Prodi's government was re-constituted one day later.

A VERY STILL LIFE

Few great artists have been so closely associated with a particular place as Giorgio Morandi is with Bologna. He was born in Bologna, lived in Bologna, hardly ever left Bologna and died in Bologna. In 1915 he had to go to Parma, all of 50 miles away, to do his military service, but he soon fell seriously ill and went back to Bologna. In summer he would escape the city heat in Grizzana, a little village in the nearby hills. He would sometimes go to Venice, Florence or Milan to see an exhibition, but even these cities are near enough for the journey to be made there and back in a day. He rarely went as far as Rome, and only near the end of his life did he ever, very briefly, venture outside Italy, once to see an exhibition in Switzerland, once to Paris.

In Bologna itself his paintings were all done in his tiny studio, where he painted his still lifes (usually the same collection of bottles, over and over again). His townscapes were usually of the view from his window, or of his garden. Some of his landscapes at Grizzana were actually done from the house with the aid of a telescope. This isn't quite as bizarre as it sounds because a telescope has the effect of flattening the subject matter, abolishing the focal depth, giving the trees and buildings the appearance of all being on one plane, like the bottles lined up on a table in his still lifes. And the telescope and the shimmering summer heat blurred outlines, muted tonal contrasts and bleached colours just as did the dust that built up a velvety texture on the bottles, glasses, vases and other simple still life objects that he picked up in the weekly Piazzola bric-à-brac street market.

Outside his studio he even confined himself as far as possible to only a small part of Bologna. His places of employment were always in walking distance of the via

Fondazza, the street where he was born and died and where he lived with his three sisters, all of them unmarried. By the time he died Morandi's fame was world-wide as "the painter of bottles" (though in fact nearly a quarter of his works were landscapes) but in Bologna he was known, and is still known, as "the painter of Fondazza".

When a newspaper asked Morandi for an autobiographical note he sent only a few words: "I was born in Bologna in 1890 and studied at the Academy in the same city, where I now teach engraving. I paint and engrave landscapes and still lifes." He then names three magazines he has done work for, and three critics who have written about him. And that's all.

In fact his life was not quite so uneventful as that bare account suggests. For one thing, when he was 39 he stopped teaching in primary schools, and taught at the Bologna School of Art instead. Four years later there was another upheaval. At the age of 43 he left his birthplace at via Fondazza 34 and moved next door to via Fondazza 36.

Via Fondazza is a modest artisanal street with workshops and garages. Like everywhere in Bologna it has quiet, dignified, cool arcades painted in red, ochre and other earth colours — forms and a chromatic and tonal range that find themselves in Morandi's bottles, vases and bowls and the shapes between them. The shapes between become more and more important in his work until it is almost as though Morandi is painting what *isn't* there.

Morandi said that even a still life is architecture, and his still lifes are like nothing so much as the architecture of Bologna. The tall thin bottles remind us that Bologna was known as the city of a hundred towers: two leaning towers still dominate the city centre. The columns and arches of Bologna's arcades make rectangles and semi-circles as abstract as the geometry of Morandi's paintings.

Like Morandi's paintings the arcades are not as repetitive as they sound when described, and they are never monotonous. On the contrary the slight variations in shape, colour and style are capable of as infinite a number of permutations as the positions in chess. The chess analogy can be taken further. No chesspiece has importance in itself. What matters is its relation to the other pieces. Any move changes the position. In the same way the views through the columns and arches of the arcades of Bologna are always changing as you walk through them. The variations in the positions of the components of a series of Morandi's paintings are sometimes almost imperceptible but once you are attuned to the language of Morandi the slight move of a wine bottle can make as much difference as the queen moving one square in a chess-game, or redrawing a line on the map of a continent.

It was siesta time on a hot Sunday afternoon in June when I visited the via Fondazza, almost one hundred years to the day after Morandi (1890-1964) was born there. I was taking a photograph of the undistinguished exterior of number 36 when the front door opened and a man came out. I thought my behaviour must look a bid odd and crossed the road to explain why I was taking a photograph of his house. The man's face lit up. Oh yes, Signor Morandi. He knew Signor Morandi well. He had been Signor Morandi's downstairs neighbour. He invited me in. The Emilians are famous for their hospitality. They say you can tell when you're in Emilia because if you are thirsty they give you wine.

Signor Morandi and his sisters used to live upstairs. The Morandi apartment is shut up now but Signor Buselli took me into the garden where there is a big olive tree. He told me it had been planted by Signor Morandi himself and is the only olive tree in Bologna. Or is it the biggest olive tree in Bologna? My Italian let me down there.

Bruno Buselli told me that Signor Morandi never had a telephone or a radio. As for television... he lifted his hands in horror. If someone wanted to speak to Signor Morandi on the phone the call would come to Signor Buselli downstairs. Sometimes, he said, there would be a phone call from Roma. And sometimes a visitor would arrive in a car with Roman number plates. The man would stay for an hour or so and leave with some of Signor Morandi's pictures. Sometimes, he said, there had been phone calls from America.

He said that it was only in the last ten years of his life that he had realised that Signor Morandi was famous. In fact as far as Signor Buselli is concerned the extent of Morandi's fame still doesn't seem to have quite sunk in. He told me proudly that there was a big Morandi exhibition on in Bologna at the moment and was delighted to learn that this exhibition was what I had come all the way from England to see. It was still further proof of Signor Morandi's fame.

Stanley Spencer, who was born only a few months after Morandi, was as attached to the Berkshire village of Cookham as Morandi was to Bologna. When Spencer studied at the Slade he went up to London on the 8.50 train each day and came back on the 5.08. He said that when he left the Slade and went back to Cookham, he entered "a kind of earthly paradise. Everything seemed fresh and to belong to the morning." The war took him to Greece as an orderly in the Royal Army Medical Corps and in the Second World War he went to the ship-building yards of Glasgow as an Official War Artist. Otherwise his imaginative world was Cookham. Even his religious scenes are set in Cookham.

But there are big differences between Spencer and Morandi. An obvious one is that Spencer's pictures are much larger. As far as I know the tall, lean Morandi never painted a picture larger that could easily be picked up with one hand. Tiny Stanley Spencer painted some really enormous pictures. (In the same way in André Maurois's children's story Fattypuffs play Finnifer instruments like the piccolo, whereas Finnifers play Fattypuff instruments like the tuba and the bass drum.)

Another difference is that Spencer's canvasses are crowded with human beings. Throughout his life he painted portraits and self-portraits, some of them in intimate (indeed genital) detail. Morandi's landscapes, by contrast, never have human beings or even animals in them (or indeed any recognisably twentieth-century artifacts). He never painted commissioned portraits, and only rarely of his family and close friends. There are only a handful of self-portraits and in these his rather stubborn features are mostly in shadow.

In a sense Stanley Spencer's paintings are all about himself; Cookham is an extension of him, he of Cookham. Morandi's paintings are unpeopled and impersonal, the landscapes could as easily be of Normandy as Emilia, the townscapes could be any old walls and roofs, the bottles could as easily have come from a junk-shop in Brussels as Bologna. Yet, it seems to me, Morandi's paintings are, in imaginative terms, all self-portraits, all pictures of Bologna. At the same time they are outside time and place and have the impersonality of great art. For all his apocalyptic visions, Spencer is a provincial artist.

Morandi is anything but provincial. He particularised to such an extent that he enables us to glimpse fragments of universal verity as do only the greatest artists. Cesare Pavese could have been thinking of his contemporary Morandi when he said that the most certain way of amazing oneself is to stare fixedly at the same object which will miraculously seem as though we had never seen it before. The critic Franchi spoke of Morandi painting "inert objects on the beauty of which an entire eternity of placid contemplation has elapsed". Morandi himself said that "everything is a mystery, ourselves and the simplest, humblest things". He did not go along with interpretations of his pictures that gave them metaphysical, surrealist, psychological or literary meaning.

As one would expect, Morandi was not a political animal. Between the wars his work was taken up by a group of painters called the Strapaese who had right-wing leanings, and he has sometimes been tarred with their brush. The catalogue of the recent Tate Gallery "On Classic Ground" exhibition states flatly that "Morandi was sympathetic to the Fascist party, certainly through the 1920s."

I don't know what evidence there is for this serious accusation, and the catalogue immediately back-tracks on its "certainly" by saying that "in a sense, the intimacy and non-declamatory purity of his work can be seen as being opposed to the ethos of the regime," and that "it is far from clear to what extent, if any, Morandi shared the ideals of this movement (the Strapaese)." In which case the catalogue would have done better to remain silent on a subject about which it is apparently ignorant. Anyway, the Strapaese group were conservative rather than Fascist. It is true that Mussolini bought one of Morandi's still lifes, but Morandi can hardly be blamed for that. It would make just as much sense to call him a Communist because the last years of his life were spent under a Communist administration, which incidentally has handsomely honoured him with his own museum. It strikes me as guilt by association of the worst kind and that the Tate Gallery owes Morandi an apology.

Morandi resolutely, heroically, remained his own man, imperviously calm amongst the turmoil of this hyperactive century. Eduoard Roditi, who interviewed Morandi and was obviously greatly impressed by him in person, picks on what might be just a tiny inconsistency. Morandi had said he had never been willing to accept the responsibilities of teaching and giving advice, yet he had taught etching for many years. Morandi replied: "I accepted to teach etching because it implies exclusively the teaching of techniques." He was as much a master of economy in words as he was in paint. There's a well thought-out argument behind that reply. Technique you can teach. Anything beyond that is an intrusion on the individual. He respected the privacy of others as much as he expected his own to be. This is probably why he painted so few portraits. It was simply a matter of good manners.

Fastidiousness of that degree is as valuable as it is rare. Morandi was urbane and civilised. He was a man of the *urbs*, the city, Bologna. He was a man who was a *civis*, a citizen who knew that the way for people to live in high concentrations is by being civil, civilised. By contrast Stanley Spencer is a rough unmannered country bumpkin, a wonderfully gifted painter but finally a bore who buttonholes us with his sexual and religious obsessions.

Roditi describes Morandi at the age of 68 as being a tall, grey-haired and scholarly man, who "avoided, in his dress and manner, everything that might suggest an artist's reputedly Bohemian way of life. True to the traditions of the North Italian middle class of the provincial cities, he was leading the same kind of restricted social life as most of the older university professors and professional men of his native city, but with an additional touch of purely personal modesty, shyness and asceticism." Morandi said "I suppose I remain a believer in art for art's sake rather than art for the sake of religion, of social justice or of national glory." Roditi felt himself to be in the presence of "a sage, if not a saint".

Bologna is red brick rather than stucco or marble. It has the reputation of being cut off from the rest of Italy, practical, solid, down-to-earth rather than *bella figura*. Morandi and Bologna are aristocratic in their aloofness, their disdain of fame. "I have always led a very quiet and retiring life and never felt much urge to compete with other contemporary painters, whether in terms of production or of exhibitions."

You don't need to compete when you know you're the best. Milton said that fame is the spur, the last infirmity of the noble mind. Picasso had it badly, Morandi not at all.

Morandi was born within days of van Gogh's killing himself. No two artists could be more different, in their lives or in their art. While van Gogh's life would have been the stuff of Hollywood even if his paintings had been without merit, Morandi's was so quiet as to be almost invisible. While van Gogh shouts almost deafeningly, Morandi commands our attention with a whisper.

Over-exposure of van Gogh's biography has created a real barrier in looking at his paintings. There is no such danger in Morandi's case. He belongs not to the companionship of Michelangelo but Vermeer. Or Gogol, in Nabokov's tender description: "True poetry of that kind provokes not laughter and not tears — but a radiant smile of perfect satisfaction, a purr of beatitude — and a writer may well be proud of himself if he can make his readers, or more exactly some of his readers, smile and purr that way." A purr of beatitude. Bologna. Morandi.

Guardian, *November 24, 1990*

CHANGE IN THE VILLAGE

Reports of the Death of the English Village have been coming in for quite some time now. When I was at Cambridge in the late 1950s, an enormously influential book was *Culture and Environment* by F.R. Leavis and Denys Thompson. It lamented the disappearance of the Old England. This was not in any way to be confused with the Olde England of the Ye Olde Tea Shoppe kind. Leavis's lectures were an acquired taste but highly addictive, persuasive and entertaining. Scorn and derision he poured in equal quantities on Morris dancers. "Bells on their knees," he would say, and we would fall about laughing. No, the real Old England was the one where the village was an Organic Community, and it had disappeared only very recently. Dr Leavis could remember when, in Cambridge market, butter would be cut from a great slab and not wrapped in grease-proof paper but in a cabbage leaf. Under Leavis's spell that cabbage leaf seemed very important.

That was 30 years ago, but the book in which Leavis and Thompson set out their case was published in 1932, and most of its evidence came from George Sturt's *Change in the Village*, which was published in 1911 at which time Sturt said that rural England is "dying out now".

In one of the least-known but (in my view) most interesting works of the late Raymond Williams, *The Country and the City*, he follows this vanishing horizon into the past. Before Leavis there was Sturt. Before Sturt there was Hardy writing in the 1880s and harking back to the rural England of the 1830s, as had George Eliot earlier in *The Mill on the Floss* and *Felix Holt*. But in the 1820s Cobbett was beefing on about how much better rural England was when he was a lad in the 1780s, and John Clare in 1809 wrote of "those golden years" of the 1790s. And in *The Village* (1783) Crabbe tells us how things aren't what they were in his day which would have been about 1769 when Goldsmith was writing "The Deserted Village". Well, if you want to you can go back to Chaucer and Piers Plowman, and thence to Virgil and ultimately to the Garden of Eden where no doubt Adam and Eve spent their time moaning on about how much better village life was before the Big Bang.

Discussing the Death of the English Village really is a bit like the Hunting of the Snark. So what kind of a Boojum does this elusive creature turn out to be? Is it dead, or dying, or in the process of yet again transforming itself? Is it (whatever it may be that we are talking about) a Good Thing or a Bad Thing? Is this Boojum (or Snark) a local phenomenon, a national one or a global one? Marshall McLuhan used to talk about the Global Village, but I'm supposed to be talking about the English village, but in the global village everything is interconnected and a sneeze here causes an earthquake there. My head's going round.

Let's think about rubbish. When I was a small boy living in the country in the years just after the war, there didn't seem to be very much rubbish. If there had been it would probably either have been taxed or rationed like everything else. Nowadays rubbish is everywhere except where it should be and is a major problem. Nuclear rubbish is a global problem. With great cities and industrial plants it is a national or even international one. Even in rural areas where people have open fires in the house and bonfires outside and compost heaps as well, it is still a problem.

It may not be much of one by the standards of the nuclear industry but for us it is still a problem.

Twenty years ago (or "one score year come damsel-tuppin' time", as we say here in Mummerset, leaning against a gate with straws in our mouths and complaining about the price of smocks), 20 years or so ago when I first came to live in a small (pop. 250-300) village on the Berkshire Downs, we put the rubbish in the traditional metal dustbins which look like squat Corinthian columns with fluted sides and lids which a kid could use as a shield in one hand while waving a wooden sword in the other.

Then the Council announced that they would take away our old dustbins free of charge and replace them (also free of charge) with wire contraptions like upwardly-mobile supermarket baskets with a gadget at the top for holding a black plastic bag. They weren't big enough, they were top-heavy, fell over and spilled the contents, or else rats made short work of the black plastic and spread the rubbish all around.

The Council next came up with wheely-bins. (Stay with me and you'll find that this is all absolutely relevant to the English Village, Death of.) Wheely-bins proved to be ingeniously designed, easily manoeuvred, capacious, hardwearing, and with lids that fit tightly enough to keep flies and other pets out (I intended to write pests but pets will do) and to keep stinks in. I was hostile to the wheely-bin at first, but I confess to being now a convert.

On Fridays we all wheel out our wheely-bins into the road and there they are ready for collection and inspection. Whether it is to stop them being nicked or so that the dustmen won't get them mixed up, most people paint on the bin the name of the house it belongs to. Written on mine is "the old skool" (s back-to-front of course) because I live in what was the village school until about 30 years ago. When it closed the children were put into buses and taken long distances to various schools around the area.

The closing down of village schools in this half of the century has contributed considerably to the destruction of the village as a community. Nowadays it is not hard to find villages which have no school, no shop, no pub: in fact they have become no more than a huddle of houses. There is nothing to bring people together, there is no community. In my village we are lucky in still having two pubs, a village hall, and a sub-post-office-cum-village shop where you can buy everything from newspapers and provisions to fresh fruit and vegetables (local produce in season), shoe polish or aspirins.

In my village, as I have said, the school is closed and since there are only half a dozen children on the school bus each morning it is clear that the school could not have kept going, even if its catchment area extended far out from the parish. When the school was built, 150 years ago, it must have been intended for at least 60 children. This lends support to what is sometimes claimed, that the population of the English village is now lower than at any time since the Black Death.

But back to the rubbish. The wheely-bin next door is marked The Old School House, where, in living memory, the two school-marms lived. Other wheely-bins in the village include The Old Inn, The Old Forge and the Old Vic (nothing to do with the theatre but the former Vicarage) and the Old Chap (the Old Chapel). As for other parts of the country I find that my address book soon reveals that I know people who live variously in The Old Mill, The Old Post Office, The Old Bakery and The Old Mission Hall. This is all evidence of the changing use of buildings and the disappearance of trades and occupations. Other wheely-bins and addresses are less immediately revealing, but in fact Rose Cottage, Yew Tree Cottage and Bankside (to name three near-neighbours) all used to be farmworkers' cottages and are now inhabited either by commuters or week-enders.

This doesn't mean that there's no work in the village any more. I happen to know that the chap who lives in the Old School does virtually all his work there. Thanks to modern technology there is really very little need for me to go in to the *Guardian,* which is something I do mostly for social reasons and to show my face and remind people that I still exist. My neighbour in the Old School House used to spend three hours a day driving to and from his place of work. Now (again thanks to modern technology) he runs a business from home exporting soft drinks to the Middle East. The Old Post Office people run a mail-order wine business from home. The Old Baker compiles indexes for publishers. And so on. There are all sorts of white-collar cottage industries. Though its nature may have changed there is still plenty of work done in the English village.

Nevertheless, there will be some who use my wheely-bins and address book as evidence to argue that the rightful native agricultural working population has been ousted by brash urban yuppies. It's not like that at all. This was happening before the yuppies, or even the parents of the yuppies, were born. From the 1930s, if not earlier, the charming thatched cottage in easy reach of London looked very attractive to the professional car-owning classes.

After the war an extensive programme of council housing was carried out. This was often unimaginative, usually consisting of rows of identical stucco, semi-detached dwellings. But they were soundly built, spacious, had running water, electricity and inside toilets. Farm workers and their families were only too delighted to get out of their charming thatched cottages where you have to duck every time you go through a doorway (I know: I lived in one for five years), where there's no proper heating, no mod cons, the toilet is at the end of the garden (not much fun on a cold and windy night) and as often as not there were two families with numerous children living in what is now a cosy nook for a young couple and their little darling. And another and not unimportant change is that, when farm workers lived there, these were tied cottages. That is to say, they went with the job. If you lost your job (through ill-health, old age or on the whim of the farmer) you lost your house.

The rosy-tinted view of rustic life tends to forget this and other such things as the forelock-tugging deference to the gentry. And the village idiots who were a staple joke in *Punch* from about 1880 to 1940. Did nobody pause to ask themselves why there were village idiots? Before the bicycle these village communities were terribly inbred, and no one will ever know what was the incidence of incest in those desperately overcrowded charming little thatched cottages. Anyone who has a romantic idea of the village life of Old England should read *Lark Rise to Candleford* and *Akenfield* for starters.

So much for rubbish. Now let's try trees. One of the things that first attracted me to the village was the trees. The beech woods were magnificent, and in the churchyard stood a massive yew tree well over a 1,000 years old (it is in fact the yew tree Tennyson writes about in one of his finest poems, the opening of "In Memoriam"). The village green was called Nine Elm Green for obvious reasons. Big fields were lined with rows of towering elms that were probably planted as boundary lines at the time of the Enclosure Acts. The village cricket field was surrounded by three concentric rings of massive elms which gave the impression of the aisles of some circular arboreal Gothic cathedral. John Betjeman said the village had the finest collection of elms in the country.

Well, along came Dutch Elm disease, and then there were none. The massive yew tree came down in a spectacular storm, leaving a splinter (by its standards, a reasonable tree by normal ones) which survives with various props, crutches and buttresses. And then the hurricanes of 1988 and 1989 smashed motorway-width swathes through the beech woods. Fortunately they are being replanted and as I write (late April) the sky-blue carpets of bluebells lift the heart, but the woods won't be the same for at least another century.

What happened to the trees came through natural causes — or acts of God, as the theologically perceptive insurance people call them. Acts of man have brought about far greater changes. The first major change in the scene came with the agricultural revolution — Jethro Tull, Turnip Townsend and the Enclosures. The next big shock was the Depression of the 1930s, with all its delapidation, followed by the horrifying discovery at one point in the war that we were within a matter of days of running out of food, in spite of rigorous and efficient rationing (a week's ration was less than many people eat at a single meal nowadays).

It was decided after the war that we must be far more self-reliant and less dependant on imported food. This policy was followed through energetically and in some ways very successfully. But there was a price to be paid. Mechanisation meant a smaller labour force. In the name of efficiently, farming units became bigger and bigger. The children's idea of old MacDonald's farm had pigs and cows and geese and ducks and hens and sheep and pasture and cornfields and reliable old cart horses. That wasn't efficient. Specialise, specialise. And so we got mono-culture. One crop. The same crop. Year after year. Traditionalists said this would exhaust the soil. Well, pour on nutrients. Pour on pesticides. Pour on insecticides.

Those of us who objected in the 1960s were called all sorts of horrid things. Luddites was the mildest insult. We pointed out that even if the farmers were producing more food the import bill was colossal since we were importing fertilisers, chemicals, fish meal and so on instead of food. And we pointed out that the landscape was being terribly damaged. DDT was the worst but not the only offender, but combined with mono-culture, the ripping out of hedgerows and various other innovative examples of agricultural progress, the flora and flora were being destroyed in ways which in many cases are irreversible. But it was hard to get anyone very excited by such topics as soil erosion. (I think I'm right in saying that it takes 1,000 years to make an inch of top soil: I'm sure I'm right in saying that it can be lost in a year.) And who would want to complain that there were far fewer flies in the house, or wasps at a picnic? There were not many who even noticed that the cricket no longer sang in the hearth, or the grasshopper no longer croaked in the long grass in summer, or that it was a long time since they saw stoats and weasels and slow-worms and frogs, or bats at dusk or heard owls at night. Indeed, for me some of those things are only memories, and they belong to my childhood rather than adolescence. The only time I ever saw a glow-worm in England was when I was about ten. In Hardy's novel *The Return of the Native* they were plentiful enough for the two dice-players to collect them to light their game at night.

And then came the Common Market. Everyone hates the Common Market in general and its agricultural policy in particular. My objections seem to be different from those of most people, and they have to do with the way the cash has been doled out. In Britain it went to the "efficient" farmers, and that means the big ones, who have in some parts of the country created prairie landscapes that are a short step from desertification. The most recent figures to hand show that the 12 per cent of largest farms account for 57 per cent of the agricultural land use while the 45 per cent of small farmers get only 2.6 per cent. To put it simply, the little chaps are little and the big chaps are simply ENORMOUS. And guess who gets the lolly.

Meanwhile in France, for example, the cash went to the "inefficient" farmers, the small farmers. These are the people who maintain the way of life that so many of us go to France on holiday to enjoy, where the smallest village has at least one bakery, two charcuteries, local cheeses, wines, fresh produce, local specialities, splendid meals at affordable prices.

And now it's all changing. I fear the supermarkets are making their inroads in France. And here we see weird signs of attempts to reverse course. There are farmers going organic. There is something called set-aside, which means the farmer is paid not to use his land. There are attempts to turn farms into leisure centres or make use of them as "amenities", or wild-life sanctuaries. And as I sit at my word-processor in my Old School I can just see through the window on a hillside in the distance a smudge of a line: they are replanting the hedge that I remember them grubbing out 20 years ago.

The above first appeared in the Guardian Earth Supplement *for the Rio Conference in June 1992.*

STARKNESS AT NOON

Dawn has broken and the little town is slowly coming to life. A thin cat treads its delicate way across the street while a middle-aged man with a small moustache and a big belly walks sedately back from the baker's shop with a still-warm loaf under his arm.

The scene is identical to that in every other town or village in France at this time of day. There's just one difference. Like the cat, the man with the loaf under his arm hasn't got any clothes on.

Such is the poverty in the Mediterranean that in recent years many of the women, especially the younger ones, have been able to afford only half a swimming costume. Here in Cap d'Agde they are so wretchedly poor that they can't afford clothes at all.

Nowadays nudist beaches are as plentiful as blackberries, but Cap d'Agde doesn't just have a nudist beach, nor is it just a nudist resort. No, Cap d'Agde is a nudist *town*. People go about their daily routine just like anywhere else, doing their shopping, cashing cheques at the bank, sitting in cafes, buying bread, playing tennis, eating in restaurants and chatting on street-corners — without any clothes on. Starkers.

Fifteen years ago there were just a few little cottages in this part of Cap d'Agde. Then it was declared a clothes-free zone, Port Nature. The town's official guide says that the naturist village "...soon became the resort's powerhouse. Indeed, right the first year, some 2,200 families, most of them (Belgians and Germans) not hesitating to travel the nearly 15,200 kilometres at a time when the expressways weren't yet laid."

Now that the expressways have got laid the clientele has become yet more cosmopolitan, "coming from Japan or South America". And many other countries too, including

France itself of course. The population grows to something like 40,000 during the season. The original small houses that survive are now dominated by huge complexes of semi-circular ziggurats which make the place look as though the University of East Anglia has come down to the seaside and had kittens, except that the kittens have grown up to be far larger than the cat.

Fat cats too. It's soon apparent that, after all, the lack of clothes does not come from poverty. It is only in the literal sense that the residents are not well-heeled; the middle-aged ones are people of substance in more than one way, and the younger ones include a high proportion of the BCBG *(Bon chic, bon genre)* and what in the Eighties we called Sloane Rangers and yuppies.

On the beach itself the rules are strict. No dogs. No cameras. Clothes are permitted, but the local etiquette dictates that if the ambient temperature is such that you feel you really have to wear something, then you put the garment on your top half. Rather than go topless, you go bottomless. It has to get quite chilly before you cover up your willy.

* * *

Packing for the journey to the Cap was the work of a moment. No need to spend a long time selecting suitable items from the wardrobe. But if I found myself travelling light on clothes I was weighed down by something far more cumbersome. Trepidation.

It's many years since I left school. Since then I have rarely seen a naked man, and to the best of my knowledge no man has seen me totally nude. When I go to a swimming bath and take a shower afterwards I keep my swimming trunks on. All right, I'm a prude. I have, so to speak, a hang-up about other blokes looking at my cock. Yes, yes, I know what you're going to say. In my time I too have read books by the Viennese quack (as Nabokov called Freud), but the knowledge that deep analysis might prove me to be a repressed homosexual didn't make it any easier on the way to Cap d'Agde.

Trains on French railways are wonderfully smooth and the sleepers are luxuriously comfortable. Usually I sleep better on them than anywhere else, secure in the knowledge that I'm not going to be woken by a telephone (sorry, wrong number). This time I spent a restless night, anxiously anticipating the events of the next day.

I could see it all. High Noon. A man's godda do what a man's godda do, and what I godda do's my doody (which Frankie Laine rhymes with beauty). Aneurin Bevan said he would not go naked into the conference chamber. I was going to have to go naked on to the beach. If any butterflies were reported missing that night then they were in my stomach. The thought wouldn't go away. In a few hours' time I was going to have to take all my clothes off and walk around with nothing on, in front of a lot of people half of whom would be MEN. Would I be up to it? Did I have the...? Every phrase that came into my head was loaded with innuendo.

Picture the scene. South of France, blue sky with the sun smiling down on a landscape by Bonnard. A middle-aged Englishman has just got off the train, weighed down with trepidation and blushing with an anticipatory embarrassment that he hopes he will be able to pass off as the result of a first-day's sun-bathing.

I hailed a taxi which displayed its owner's name as Sanchez. Nice chap, Sanchez. He gave me a fluent conducted tour of Agde and the route to my destination in Cap d'Agde, and then fixed up my accommodation in Port Nature. At the entrance to the nudist town there is a barrier of the kind used at level crossings and frontier borders. Non-residents have to pay 10 francs for admission but Sanchez knew the ropes and we were through with a wave and a smile.

As there are no hotels in the village, Sanchez took me to an accommodation bureau. Hardly had I started negotiating the short-term rental of a small studio flat when from a room at the back there came the sound of a distraught voice wailing into a telephone.

"*Oui* (sob, sob). *C'est Yvonne,* (sob, sob) *Bon-papa... il est... mort).*"

The room suddenly went very quiet and very cold as we listened to the tale of woe. Yes, she said, they were on holiday. Sob, sob. At Cap d'Agde. Grandpapa had been swimming in the afternoon. He had a good meal in the evening. Grandpapa had gone to bed fairly early, and then (sob and wail) DIDN'T WAKE UP IN THE MORNING. The doctor had been summoned and he had confirmed that Grandpapa was dead.

Her accent proclaimed her to be Belgian, which meant that this was long-distance. She suddenly realised this herself and in order to cut down on the cost of the call abruptly ceased the sobbing and got down to details. These were that in view of the heat the best thing was to have Grandpapa incinerated on the spot. Then she would bring the ashes back with her. In an urn. On the train. On Saturday. No, not this Saturday, the one after, of course. After the end of the holiday.

This practical approach made Sanchez and me feel better. As we headed for my new quarters we agreed that Grandpapa was a lucky man. He had had a day in the sun, on the beach, looking at pretty girls, had had a good meal and didn't wake up in the morning. Not a bad way to go.

But then, as I settled down into my tiny flat overlooking a harbour crowded with small yachts, I began to worry. It was a Tuesday morning, so Grandpapa had probably been here for only a couple of days. Mental arithmetic went into top gear. Let's say Grandpapa was half my age again. He had lasted two days. That gave me three, which was precisely the period for which I had rented the flat. There was no time to be lost.

It was a windy day. There are two cold winds in this part of France, the Mistral and the Tramontane. Since they blow from different directions you would have thought that it would be a meteorological impossibility for them both to blow at the same time. That's what I thought. I was wrong. In the words of Tennessee Ernie Ford, if the left don't get you, then the right one will.

The good thing about these cold winds was that they justified my going out into the town with trousers on. I bought a newspaper and the guide to Cap d'Agde and settled down in a cafe to watch the world go nakedly by. As I was doing so I realised to my embarrassment that my flies were undone. Dropping the newspaper onto my lap I surreptitiously zipped up. It took a moment to realise the absurdity of what I was doing in a nudist context.

To calm my nerves I ordered a pastis. I had to go through with this thing. I was going to have to go down to that beach and take all my clothes off. Why couldn't I have an easy assignment like covering a war? How do I get into these situations? With heart pounding, I ordered a second pastis. Another fine mess I'd got me into.

By way of a delaying tactic I studied the official Guide to Cap d'Agde. The publication takes an approach to the English language which is both bold and inventive. In his introduction the mayor, Pierre Leroi-Beaulieu, writes:

> Deliberately turned to the third millennium, our resort town Cap d'Agde offers you all the facilities, diversified, and harmoniously laid out on the territory, of a commune whose history merges with that of the Mediterranean. Our welcome is the fruit of a centuries-old tradition.

The Guide tells us that "You don't need to be a champion or a jogging nut to have a ball at The Cap." It is a place

> ...for all kinds of pleasures, all kinds of encounters from noon to midnight, beautiful tanned women and sun-burned ephebes 'cruise' endlessly, full of sun, calm and loving

just like the sea, available and light like the
sun offered to them.

In short, the Cap is "a lesson in liberty, respect and tolerance, where all the lovers of the Mediterranean can live their passion to the hilt, with the sun as witness."

I started making notes — as good a form of displacement activity as any. *Woman of about 65 with a stunning figure. Restaurant menus seem to be mostly in German or English. Likewise, German and English beer are prominent. This bar is selling Irish Cofee and Explosif Waikiki. Another menu offers Battered fish. Why do so many male nudists smoke pipes? Good grief, there's a man with some kind of bracelet round his penis.*

I averted my gaze and went back to the Guide.

> Those who are unconditionally into tanning on an air mattress or chaise longue, get together here in the sun like contented cats; or to simper in front of their iced drinks with a straw in their mouths. As for the athletic types who get into the wind, speed and strong feelings, they indulge freely in water ski, parascension, water scooter, etc.

Well, I had simpered long enough in front of my iced drinks. I paid up and made my way down a street past a shop where a naked girl was looking longingly at the clothes on the racks. And so to the beach, a mile of sand dotted with men, women and children, all bare. This, then, was the moment of truth.

It turned out to be not too bad. As with aeroplanes and dentists, the anticipation is the worst part. I imagined walking on the beach and everyone pointing at me and saying "Oh-la-la" or "You must be joking." Bite the bullet. Off with the trousers. Unaccommodated man is no more but such a poor, bare, forked animal as thou art. Off, off, you lendings. Come, unbutton here. Stride purposefully for the deep blue sea.

And nobody takes the slightest notice.

It's amazing how quickly you get used to it. It soon seems not only natural but normal.

How confused my attitudes are not only to the private and public appearances of my own body, but also the bodies of others, male and female, clothed and unclothed.

The conventional wisdom is that there is nothing less erotic than uncovered human beings. This is something I had learnt in my first morning in the life class at art school. The point of clothes is that you want to remove them. This girl, for example, is defying beach rules and wearing a bikini. She looks stunning. The ones without clothes reveal tattoos, appendix scars, stretch-marks, big bellies. Naked human beings are mostly not good-looking. Both sexes have too many wobbly bits. Adam and Eve were right (Genesis chapter 3, verse 7): "And the eyes of both of them were opened, and they knew that they were naked, and they sewed fig-leaves together, and made themselves aprons."

But there are exceptions to the conventional wisdom about naked bodies being un-erotic, and these can make the libido threaten to go into over-drive. Here's a girl with a pony-tail, and she's carrying an ice-cream cornet and she could well be the next Brigitte Bardot. The photographer David Hamilton used to visit the Cap frequently, and spotted many a model.

The trouble with these rare gorgeous creatures, whose sylph-like forms move with the grace of a gazelle and make a man kinda glad he was born (Frankie Laine), is that they're unobtainable. Here's Hawkeye on the beach and he spots a pretty little kitten and he's plannin' to be sittin' by her side pretty soon. Hawkeye isn't worried about his strategy, which is simplicity itself, but he's got to work out his tactics, and as an opening gambit Pawn to King's four is not good enough.

Hawkeye has just decided that he will introduce himself as David Hamilton's agent when everything goes wrong.

She is suddenly no longer alone. Her parents have joined her, a boring-looking couple of about Hawkeye's own age. Or if it's not her parents it's a man even older than them with gray hair and a resemblance to Fernando Rey; almost certainly her boss. Or else it's a muscular, bronzed athletic, dazzlingly good-looking young Adonis (or ephebe?). In any case she has company. Hawkeye tells his libido that it's just not our day.

In fact, as far as I could see, the opportunities for sexual adventure at the Cap are limited. There are couples and there are families. It all seemed extremely respectable. When nobody is wearing clothes there are few thrills either for voyeurs or exhibitionists. There are no sex shops, and the newsagents have far fewer soft-porn magazines than those that crowd the shelves of shops in most of France.

But in his wanderings round the town Hawkeye had noticed various "non-conformist" night-clubs inviting custom restricted exclusively to couples. Since Hawkeye wasn't a couple he would need a partner if he was going to penetrate one of these joints.

In the bar he frequented there was a German barmaid who had always been very friendly. As he bought a glass of wine he made a request of her, prefacing his remarks by saying he hoped she would not misunderstand his intentions. Would she, after she had finished work that night, accompany him to one of these clubs, just so that he could get in? Just to establish his bona fides. She need only stay a few minutes.

Misunderstand?! She hit the roof. She'd been working here all summer and men had been tra-la-la and then she thought at last here was someone who tra-la-la and it turned out he was just like all the rest, only interested in one thing, bang, crash, wallop, scream. In short she would not accompany me to a club.

As it turned out, it wouldn't have made any difference even if the Fraulein had been more compliant, since the clubs were shut. This was partly because it was the end of the season. Also, these "non-conformist clubs" had earned a reputation not just for *exchangisme* (wife-swapping) but also for acts of public indecency and outrages to public morals in breach of article 300 of the Penal Code.

An enthusiastic new police Commissaire had decided to crack down on the clubs which, he declared, were taking on the characteristics of Sodom and Gomorrah. The name of this policeman was Borel-Garin, but it might as well have been Clouseau. On one occasion he sent in a uniformed posse to the Cleopatre club, all waving their badges. The naked clients assumed that this was part of the floor-show and greeted them with hilarity. The police retired discomfited.

On another occasion Commissaire Borel-Garin sent a mixed couple of cops to a club called Les Boffs. They would have been plain-clothes police if they had been wearing clothes. They reported back that there were low lights in the club, slow dancing, a scene of fellation, and a fat man of about 1 metre 85 centimetres in height had been making love to a blonde woman (height unspecified).

The Commissaire decided to go for *un flag* (in flagrante delicto). He chose a good-looking lady Inspector aged 27, and a male cop of an age and rank that the report in the local newspaper did not specify. The plan was that they would enter Les Boffs at 1.30 a.m. unclothed. The rest of the police (in uniform) would form a cordon and swoop at 2.45.

The intrepid clothesless cops had hardly entered when one of the clients recognised them. He tipped off the proprietress who set about calming the ardours of the more exuberant customers. Meanwhile the sneak created a diversion by asking the policewoman for a dance. Her male colleague came to her assistance. He said that she didn't want to dance but (clenched fists) that he would. The client replied that he didn't dance with queers.

By now the hapless couple of cops, exposed in every sense, were the subject of noisy derision and abuse, and were forced to retreat under a hail of laughter and ridicule long before the hour appointed for the uniformed police to burst in.

In spite of such farcical incidents the clubs were closed down for a while, to the indignation of most of the village's bar-keepers and shopkeepers whose livelihoods depend on the naturists, who in their turn claim that there is far more propriety in the village than down the coast which they describe as a paradise for voyeurs, where they're at it all the time, even in front of the children, whereas at the Cap they do it behind closed doors.

When the time came for me to leave Cap d'Agde it felt strange to be fully clothed again. I phoned Sanchez. When he turned up he recognised me and mentioned the girl and Grandpapa's ashes. We both laughed. And laughed. And laughed. We laughed so much that we had to hold one another up. When he was able to speak Sanchez said that at least I'd survived longer than Grandpapa.

* * *

The above account is based on the cover story in the first issue of Weekend Guardian *(December 3, 1988). The cover photograph was by Nobby Clark and shows me in a deck-chair, unclothed though decently covered by the laptop on the top of my lap. Nobby skilfully suggested a seaside setting but in fact the picture was taken chez moi. The article won first prize in the International Naturism Federation press awards. The award was presented at the AGM of the British Naturism Council. Dress was informal.*